Fun & Easy
WORD BUILDING
Activities

by Mary Rosenberg

SCHOLASTIC
PROFESSIONAL BOOKS

New York • Toronto • London • Auckland • Sydney • Mexico City • New Delhi • Hong Kong • Buenos Aires

Dedication

This book is dedicated to Loraine "Mumsey" Davis
—a good friend and a great "mum" away from mom.

Edited by Lynn Mondello Caggiano

Cover design by Gerard Fuchs

Cover illustration by Rick Brown

Interior illustrations by Jane Dippold, except pages 41 and 43 by Maxie Chambliss and page 44 by Rusty Fletcher

Interior design by Ellen Matlach Hassell
for Boultinghouse & Boultinghouse

ISBN: 0-439-39501-1

6 7 8 9 10   40   09 08

Contents

Introduction

Welcome to *Fun & Easy Word Building Activities*! This easy-to-use resource is packed with hands-on games and activities that help kids strengthen reading and spelling skills easily and instantly. Kids build words in a variety of fun ways—using letter cards, cubes, and spinners—to help them learn 100 sight words and 60 word families. The activities in this book give kids practice with long and short vowels, upper- and lowercase letters, initial consonants, rhyming words, blends, and more. Each activity can be used with large or small groups, or can be placed at literacy centers for independent practice throughout the year.

Learning to manipulate language is the foundation upon which proficient reading and writing skills are built. Cracking the phonetic code, or knowing which letter or letters represent each of the 44 speech sounds found in the English language, is critical to reading achievement. Therefore, language mastery begins at the sound-letter level. The activities in this book reinforce letter and sound recognition and encourage children to play with language as they build various words. Through hands-on games and activities, children learn that by adding a letter to a word or by changing the order of the letters in a word, they can form many other words.

There are several sections in this book that each present a fun way to help children build words and develop reading skills:

Cut-and-Paste Activities challenge children to unscramble words and corresponding pictures by manipulating puzzle-like pieces.

Board Games provide reinforcement of particular vowel sounds as students build words using cards, cubes, or spinners.

Cards, Cubes, and Spinners are used with the board games but can also be used on their own in a variety of ways. Each set of reproducible cards, cubes, and spinners features six initial consonants and six word families. Children roll the cubes, spin the spinners, or manipulate the cards to form dozens of words.

Sight Words Activities help students build, recognize, and remember 100 high-frequency words.

Review Activities extend learning and provide additional reinforcement of concepts.

Fun & Easy Word Building Activities allows children to manipulate language in creative, hands-on ways. The activities and games encourage children to have fun with the sounds of language and, in the process, develop skills essential to reading success.

How to Use This Book

The activities in this book are designed for flexible use. Select the ones that best meet your students' needs and feel free to adapt them as you see fit. The activities may be used with the whole class or with small groups. You might present them as lessons on particular sounds or as reinforcement for previously learned sounds. The games and activities also work well in literacy centers and may be sent home for additional practice.

Word Lists (pages 7–9)

The word lists are divided into two categories—words with short vowels and words with long vowels. Each category is then divided into five groups—one for each vowel. Words that begin with an initial consonant are listed first, followed by words that begin with a digraph (such as *ch*, *sh*, *th*, and *wh*) or blend (such as *bl*, *br*, *sl*, *sp*, *sw*, and *tr*). On page 9, you'll find a list of common word families and sight words. Refer to the lists for words to modify or extend the activities in this book, to display in the classroom, or to create flashcards or other manipulatives for student practice.

Cut-and-Paste Activities (pages 10–33)

There are two kinds of activities in this section: Alphabet Matches and Word Scramblers. Alphabet Matches challenge children to match lower-case letters on puzzle pieces to corresponding uppercase letters on the reproducible sheet. When the pieces are arranged in the correct order, they form an illustration of a word. Each Word Scrambler includes six words that feature the same long or short vowel. The words and corresponding illustrations are scrambled. Children cut out the pieces and rearrange them to build words and pictures. Cut-and-Paste Activities are ideal for independent practice in learning centers or at home.

Board Games (pages 34–45)

The nine board games included here help children review long and short vowels. Each game includes easy-to-read directions and reproducible game boards. The Word Building Cards (pages 47–58) are used with many of the games. For a variation, have children use cubes or spinners (pages 59–84) instead of cards. The games are designed for two players and are perfect for learning centers or for practice when students are finished with other work. You might present the games following a class lesson on each sound or as a review after children have studied all the sounds. On pages 34–35, you'll find information about each game as well as suggestions for variations.

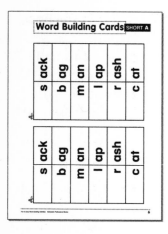

Word Building Cards (pages 46–58)

The Word Building Cards are organized by long and short vowels. Each set includes cards for six initial consonants and six word families. Children cut apart the cards and arrange them to form words. The cards are used with many of the board games, but they can also be used independently in a number of ways. Refer to page 46 for activities and games that can be played with the cards. To make additional cards, photocopy and fill in the blank card templates (page 58). As homework or guided practice, challenge students to create their own cards.

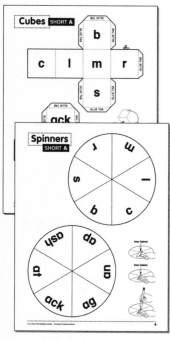

Cubes and Spinners (pages 59–84)

The reproducible cubes and spinners help children review long and short vowels as well as initial consonants and common word families. Children use either two cubes or two spinners at a time—one showing initial consonants and the other showing word families. Children either roll the cubes or spin the spinners and then determine whether they can build a word with the initial consonant and word family shown. The cubes and spinners can be used with many of the board games and can also be used on their own. Refer to pages 59–60 for activities and games using the cubes and spinners.

Sight Words Activities (pages 85–89)

Sight words, or high-frequency words, are the words most commonly encountered in any text. Often, these words do not follow regular rules of spelling, so children will not be able to easily decode them. The sight words in this book are found on the Dolch Word List, a widely recognized list of words that children must learn to recognize on sight. The words on the Dolch List account for more than 50% of the words found in textbooks today. The activities in this section reinforce the 100 words listed on page 9. Kids will build sight words using the letter cards on page 87, play Sight Word Bingo, Concentration, and more.

Review Activities and Reproducible Forms (pages 90–96)

These activities can be used as extensions for many of the activities and games in this book. You might use these activities to review concepts as needed. This section includes Word Sort, Word Ladder, and Spin a Word, as well as a Review Sheet, Word Recording Sheet, and an Activities Check-Off Sheet. The forms are provided to help students keep track of words they have formed and to help you keep track of which activities students have completed.

Short Vowel Word List

SHORT A	SHORT E	SHORT I	SHORT O	SHORT U
back	bed	bid	cob	buck
bag	bell	big	cot	bug
bat	bend	bit	dock	bump
can	bent	did	dog	bun
cap	best	dig	dot	bunk
cat	led	dip	fox	duck
lack	lend	kid	hog	jug
lag	lent	pig	hop	jump
lap	let	pill	hot	junk
man	pet	pin	job	luck
map	sell	pit	lock	lump
mash	send	quit	log	mug
mat	sent	wig	lot	pump
rack	set	will	rock	pun
rag	tell	win	rod	sum
ran	tent	wit	rot	sun
rat	test	chill	block	sunk
sack	well	chin	blot	chug
sat	went	ship	chop	chunk
black	wet	slid	shock	thump
chat	west	slip	shop	slug
that	bread	spill	slop	slump
track	shell	spin	slot	spun
trap	sled	thin	spot	truck
trash	spent	trip	trot	trunk

Fun & Easy Word Building Activities Scholastic Professional Books

Long Vowel Word List

LONG A	LONG E	LONG I	LONG O	LONG U
bake	bee	fight	cold	cube
came	deal	find	cone	cue
cage	dear	fine	cope	cute
case	deep	light	go	due
face	hear	like	gold	dune
gate	peach	line	hold	fume
hay	peak	mice	hope	fuse
lake	peel	might	joke	hue
late	peep	Mike	mold	huge
make	reach	mile	mow	June
may	real	mind	no	mule
name	seal	mine	rope	rude
say	see	nice	row	rule
take	teach	night	sold	Sue
wave	bleach	nine	told	suit
brake	bleak	rice	tone	tube
brave	cheap	right	tow	tune
flake	free	vine	blow	use
grape	sheep	bright	grow	blue
play	sleep	shine	pro	clue
shake	speak	slice	shone	flute
skate	speech	slight	show	glue
spray	sweep	spice	slope	prune
sway	teeth	spine	slow	true
tray	tree	while	throw	truth

Fun & Easy Word Building Activities Scholastic Professional Books

Word Families List

-ack	-ake	-est	-id	-ike	-op	-uck	-ule
-ag	-ale	-et	-ig	-ile	-ot	-ug	-une
-an	-ate	-each	-ill	-ind	-old	-um	-ure
-ap	-ay	-eak	-in	-ine	-one	-ump	-ute
-ash	-ed	-eal	-ip	-ob	-ope	-un	
-at	-ell	-ear	-it	-ock	-ose	-unk	
-ail	-end	-ee	-ice	-od	-ote	-ube	
-ain	-ent	-eep	-ight	-og	-ow	-ue	

Sight Words List

1. a	21. look	41. all	61. no	81. want
2. and	22. make	42. am	62. now	82. was
3. away	23. me	43. are	63. on	83. well
4. big	24. my	44. at	64. our	84. went
5. blue	25. not	45. ate	65. out	85. what
6. can	26. one	46. be	66. please	86. white
7. come	27. play	47. black	67. pretty	87. who
8. down	28. red	48. brown	68. ran	88. will
9. find	29. run	49. but	69. ride	89. with
10. for	30. said	50. came	70. saw	90. yes
11. funny	31. see	51. did	71. say	91. after
12. go	32. the	52. eat	72. she	92. again
13. help	33. three	53. four	73. so	93. an
14. here	34. to	54. get	74. soon	94. any
15. I	35. two	55. good	75. that	95. as
16. in	36. up	56. have	76. there	96. ask
17. is	37. we	57. into	77. they	97. by
18. it	38. where	58. like	78. this	98. could
19. jump	39. yellow	59. must	79. too	99. every
20. little	40. you	60. new	80. under	100. fly

Cut-and-Paste Activities

Alphabet Matches

Alphabet Matches (pages 13–22) reinforce upper- and lowercase letter identification skills. To complete a picture puzzle, students match the lowercase letter on a puzzle piece to its corresponding uppercase letter on the reproducible. When the puzzle pieces are arranged in the correct order, they form an illustration of the word. Alphabet Matches can be completed by the class or placed at a literacy center for independent practice.

Give each student a copy of the reproducible and review the directions at the top of the page. Instruct children to cut out only the letter strips and to leave the rest of the page intact. These activities feature school-related vocabulary, so you might present them as part of a back-to-school activity. Or challenge children to discover the theme that the words have in common.

▲ page 13

▲ page 14

▲ page 15

▲ page 16

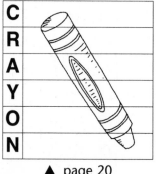
▲ page 17

▲ page 18

▲ page 19

▲ page 20

▲ page 21

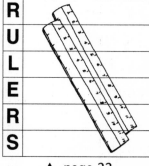
▲ page 22

Word Scramblers

Word Scramblers (pages 23–32) are a fun way to remind students that we build words to communicate ideas. As students build a word, they also create a picture illustrating the word. There are 60 Word Scramblers all together, six for each long and short vowel.

Give each student a copy of a Word Scramblers page along with the Cut-and-Paste Page on page 33. Instruct students to cut out the pieces and rearrange them to build six different words. Explain that when the letters are placed in the correct order, the pieces will form a picture illustrating the word. Also explain that the letters are used only once. Once children have formed a word, they use the remaining letters to form additional words. After children paste their pieces onto the Cut-and-Paste Page, they can color the pictures once the glue has dried. You might have children place the pieces on the sheet without gluing them. When children have finished, have them store the pieces in an envelope or small plastic bag.

> ### Learning Center Tip
> Make an enlarged photocopy of a Word Scramblers page. Then cut apart the pieces, laminate them, and place them in a pocket chart. Students can arrange the pieces to build pictures and words.

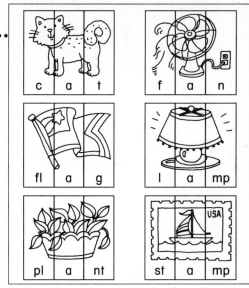

▲ page 23

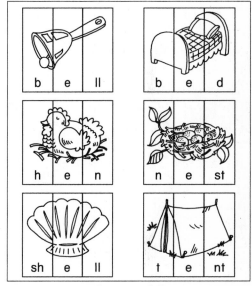

▲ page 24

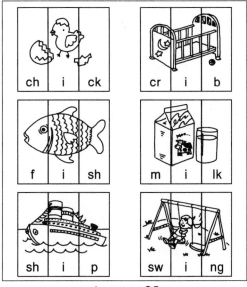

▲ page 25

▲ page 26

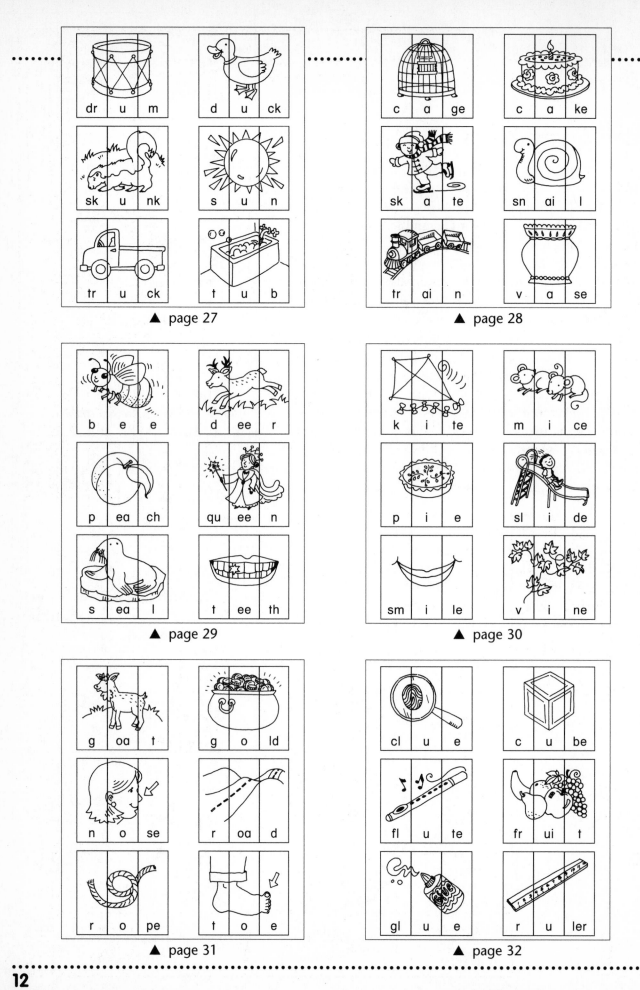

| dr | u | m |
| d | u | ck |

| sk | u | nk |
| s | u | n |

| tr | u | ck |
| t | u | b |

▲ page 27

| c | a | ge |
| c | a | ke |

| sk | a | te |
| sn | ai | l |

| tr | ai | n |
| v | a | se |

▲ page 28

| b | e | e |
| d | ee | r |

| p | ea | ch |
| qu | ee | n |

| s | ea | l |
| t | ee | th |

▲ page 29

| k | i | te |
| m | i | ce |

| p | i | e |
| sl | i | de |

| sm | i | le |
| v | i | ne |

▲ page 30

| g | oa | t |
| g | o | ld |

| n | o | se |
| r | oa | d |

| r | o | pe |
| t | o | e |

▲ page 31

| cl | u | e |
| c | u | be |

| fl | u | te |
| fr | ui | t |

| gl | u | e |
| r | u | ler |

▲ page 32

Alphabet Match

Directions: 1. Cut apart the picture strips.
2. Match the lowercase and uppercase letters.
3. Glue the strips below to form a picture.

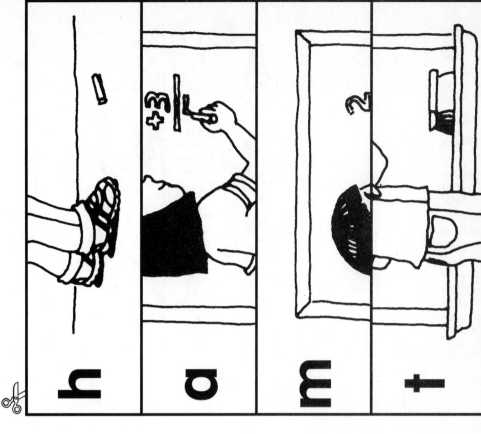

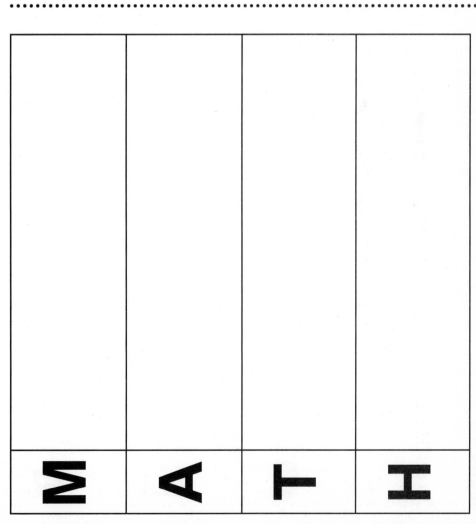

Fun & Easy Word Building Activities   Scholastic Professional Books

Alphabet Match

Directions: 1. Cut apart the picture strips.
2. Match the lowercase and uppercase letters.
3. Glue the strips below to form a picture.

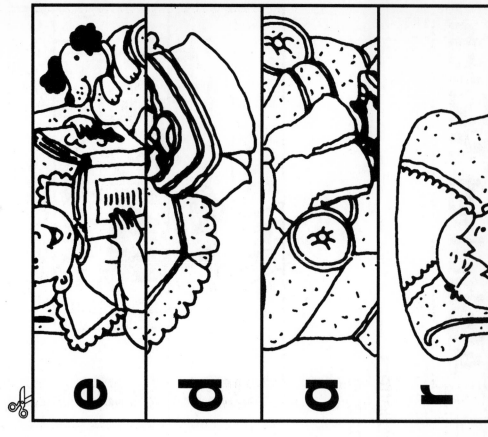

e

d

a

r

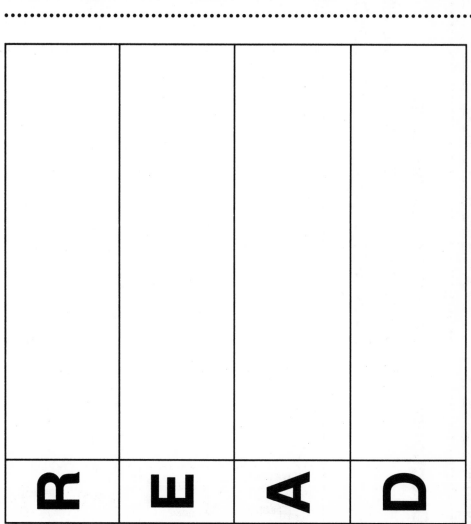

R

E

A

D

Alphabet Match

Name _____

Directions: 1. Cut apart the picture strips.
2. Match the lowercase and uppercase letters.
3. Glue the strips below to form a picture.

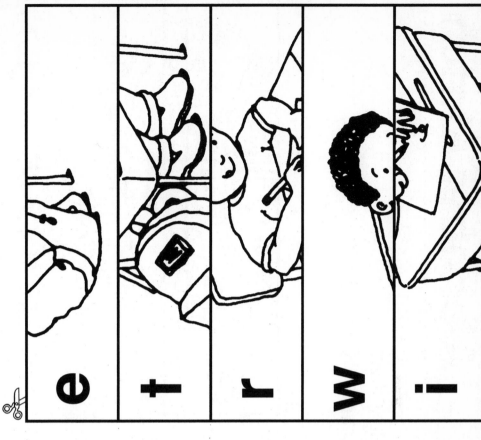

e	t	r	w	i

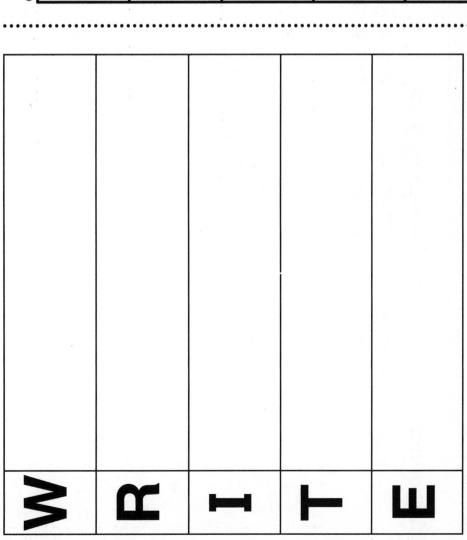

W	R	I	T	E

Fun & Easy Word Building Activities   Scholastic Professional Books

Alphabet Match

Name _____

Directions:
1. Cut apart the picture strips.
2. Match the lowercase and uppercase letters.
3. Glue the strips below to form a picture.

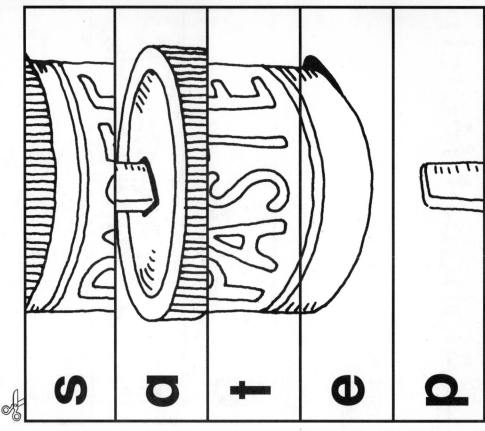

s	a	t	e	p

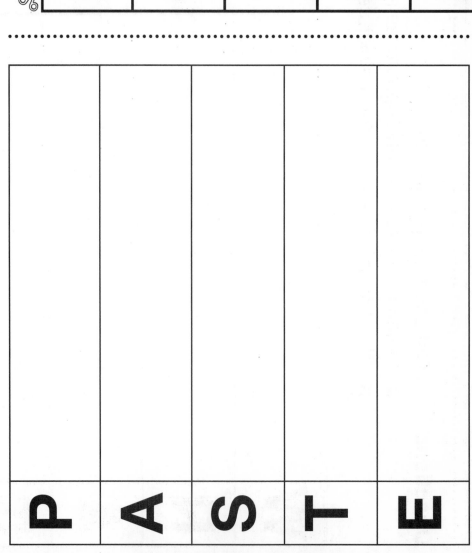

P	A	S	T	E

Fun & Easy Word Building Activities   Scholastic Professional Books

Alphabet Match

Name _____

Directions:
1. Cut apart the picture strips.
2. Match the lowercase and uppercase letters.
3. Glue the strips below to form a picture.

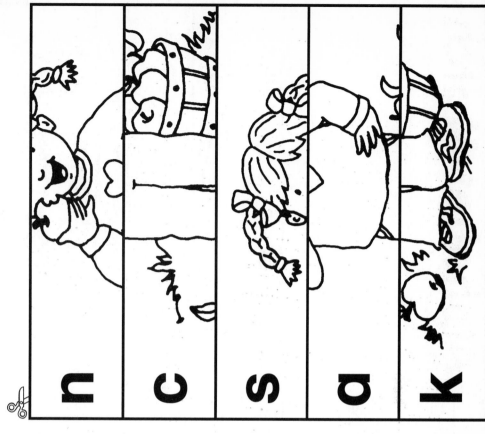

n	c	s	a	k

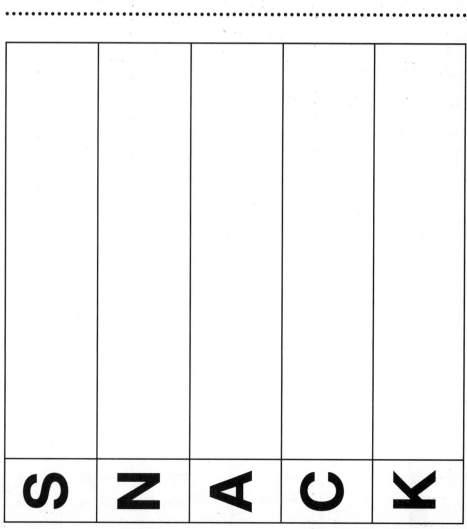

S	N	A	C	K

Fun & Easy Word Building Activities   Scholastic Professional Books

Alphabet Match

Name _____

Directions: 1. Cut apart the picture strips.
2. Match the lowercase and uppercase letters.
3. Glue the strips below to form a picture.

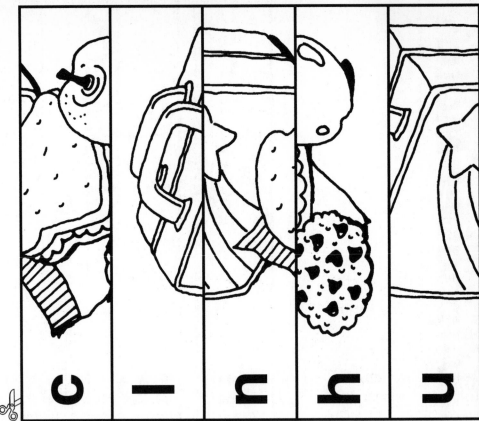

c l n h u

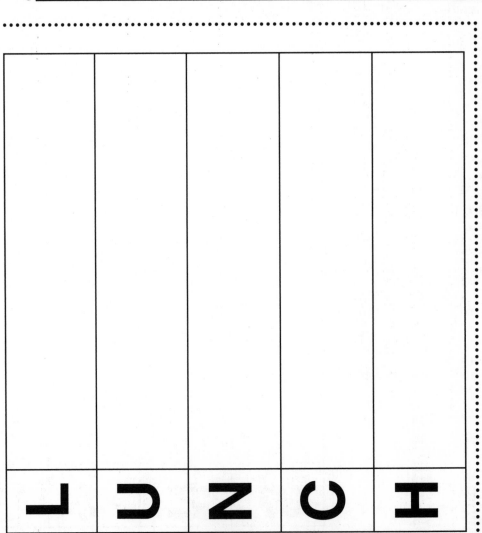

L U N C H

Fun & Easy Word Building Activities Scholastic Professional Books

Name _____

Alphabet Match

Directions: 1. Cut apart the picture strips.
2. Match the lowercase and uppercase letters.
3. Glue the strips below to form a picture.

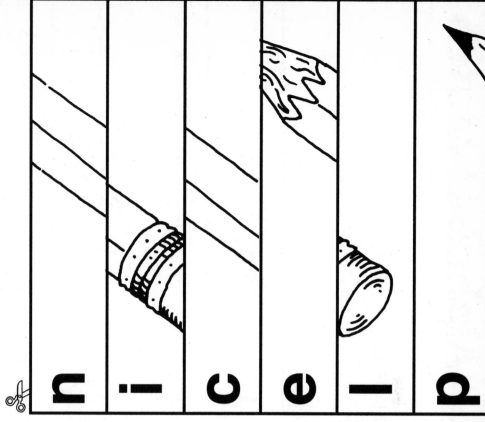

n i c e l p

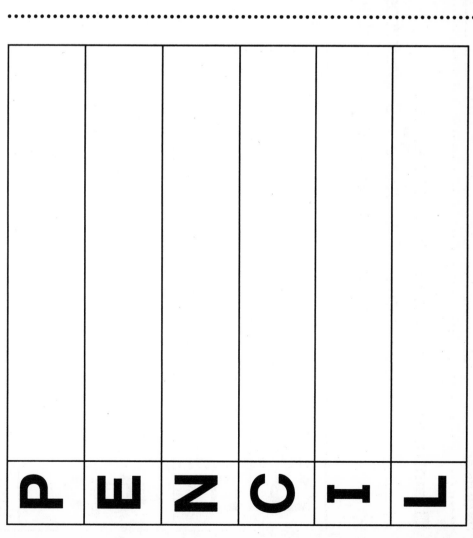

P E N C I L

Fun & Easy Word Building Activities   Scholastic Professional Books

Alphabet Match

Directions: 1. Cut apart the picture strips.
2. Match the lowercase and uppercase letters.
3. Glue the strips below to form a picture.

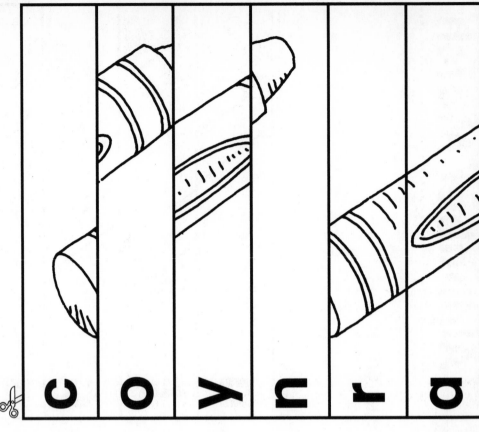

| c | o | y | n | r | a |

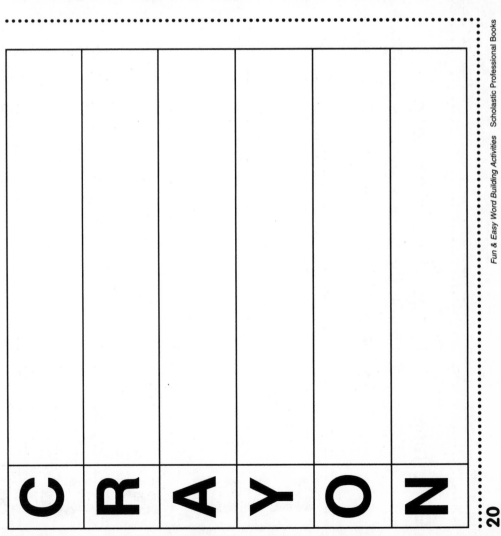

| C | R | A | Y | O | N |

Fun & Easy Word Building Activities   Scholastic Professional Books

Alphabet Match

Directions: 1. Cut apart the picture strips.
2. Match the lowercase and uppercase letters.
3. Glue the strips below to form a picture.

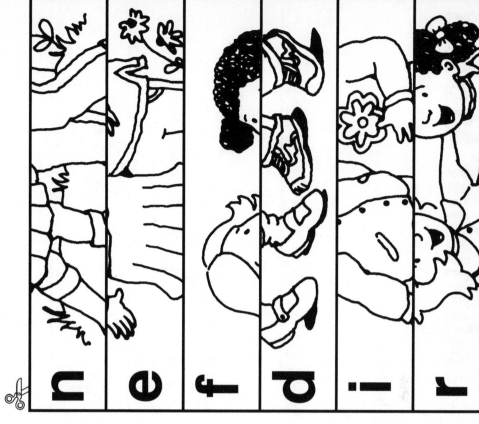

n
e
f
d
i
r

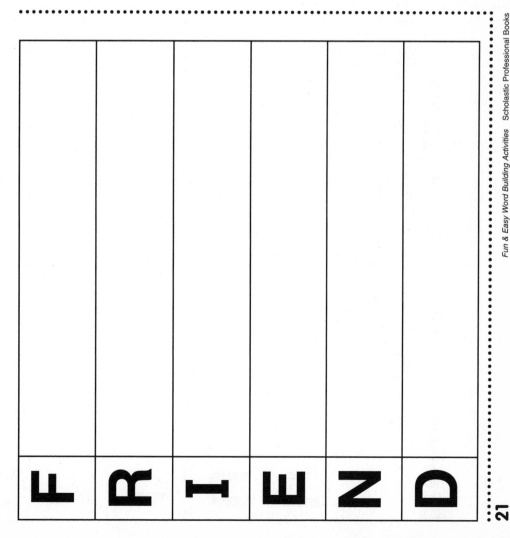

F	R	I	E	N	D

Fun & Easy Word Building Activities   Scholastic Professional Books

Alphabet Match

Directions: 1. Cut apart the picture strips.
2. Match the lowercase and uppercase letters.
3. Glue the strips below to form a picture.

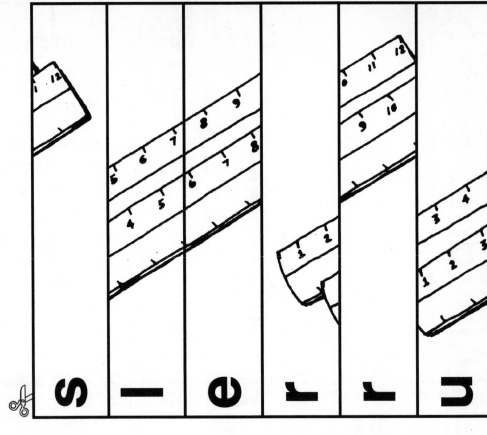

s l e r r u

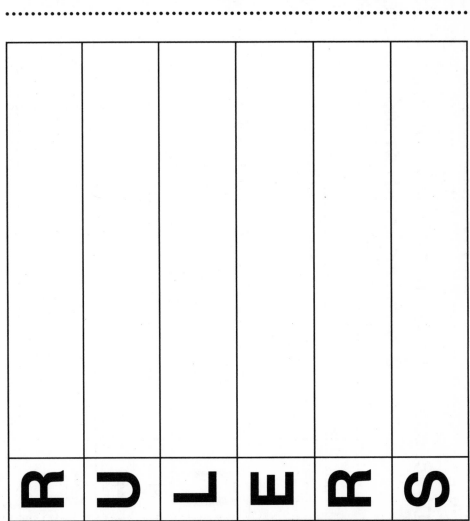

R U L E R S

Fun & Easy Word Building Activities Scholastic Professional Books

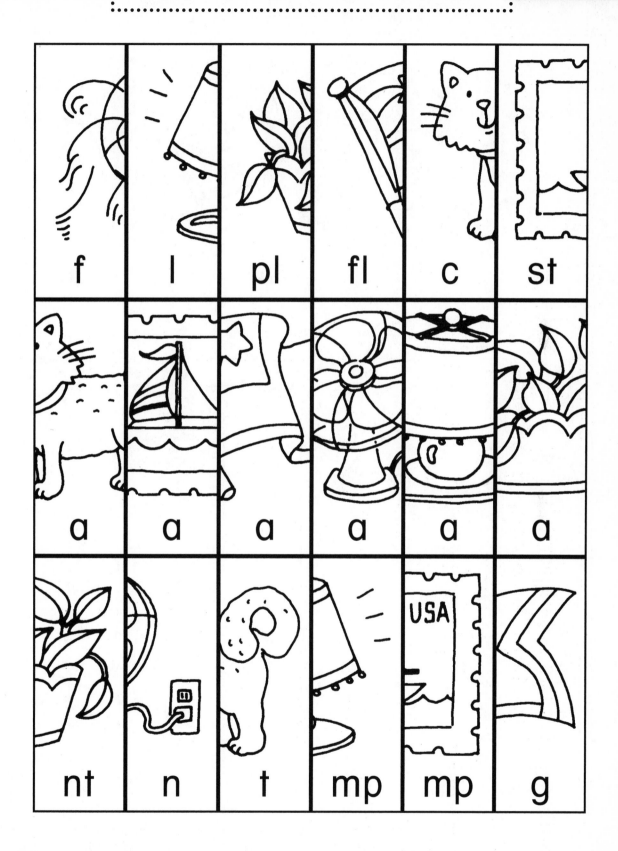

f	l	pl	fl	c	st
a	a	a	a	a	a
nt	n	t	mp	mp	g

Word Scramblers

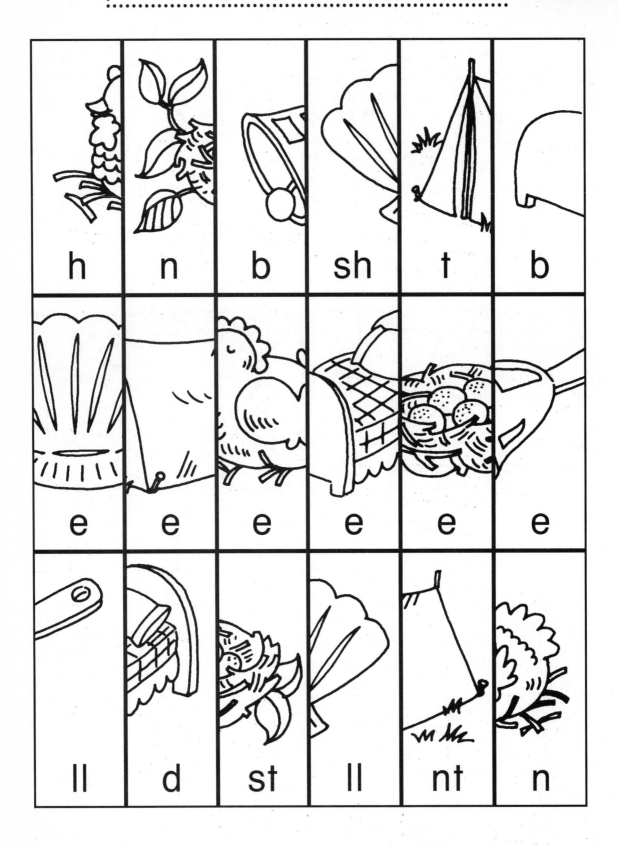

h	n	b	sh	t	b
e	e	e	e	e	e
ll	d	st	ll	nt	n

f	ch	m	sh	sw	cr
i	i	i	i	i	i
b	lk	ck	ng	p	sh

Word Scramblers SHORT O

f	d	s	fr	l	cl
o	o	o	o	o	o
ck	ck	x	ck	ll	g

Fun & Easy Word Building Activities Scholastic Professional Books

Word Scramblers

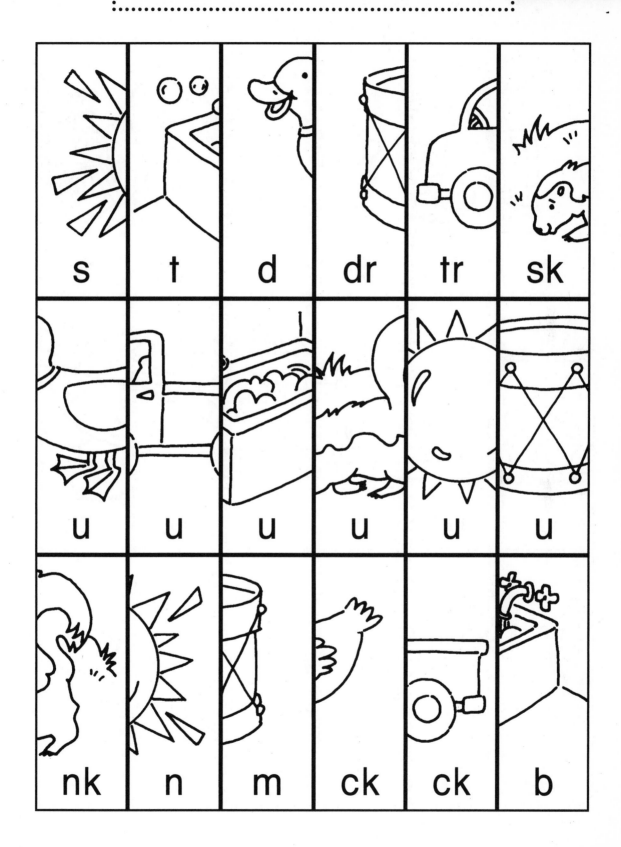

s	t	d	dr	tr	sk
u	u	u	u	u	u
nk	n	m	ck	ck	b

Word Scramblers

c	c	sk	v	sn	tr
a	ai	a	a	ai	a
ke	n	te	l	se	ge

Word Scramblers

qu	d	t	p	s	b
ee	ea	e	ee	ea	ee
e	ch	n	l	r	th

Word Scramblers

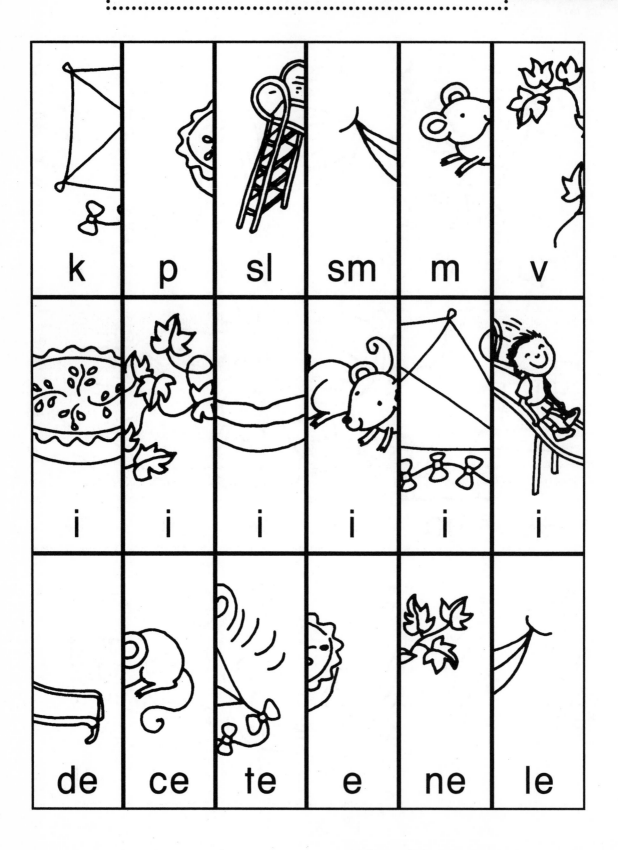

k	p	sl	sm	m	v
i	i	i	i	i	i
de	ce	te	e	ne	le

Word Scramblers LONG O

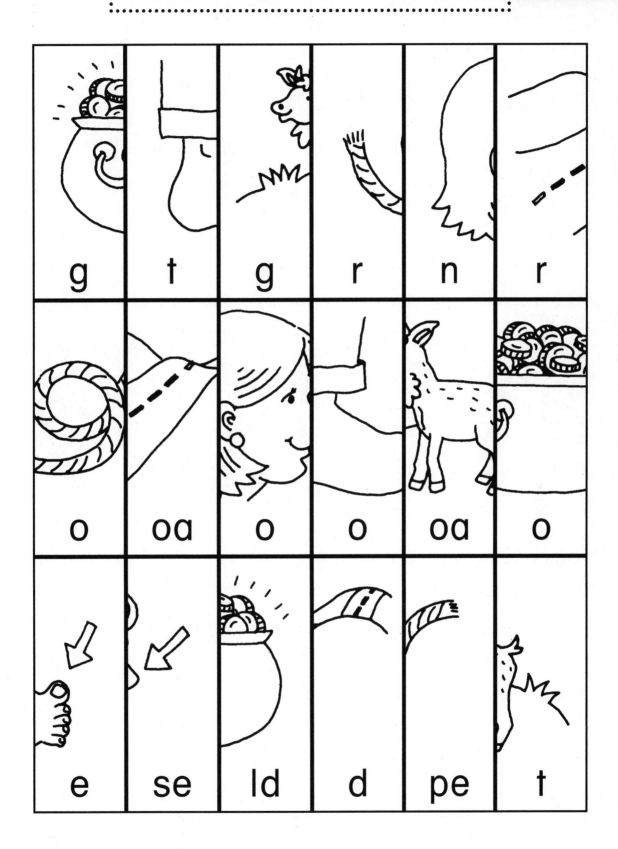

Word Scramblers

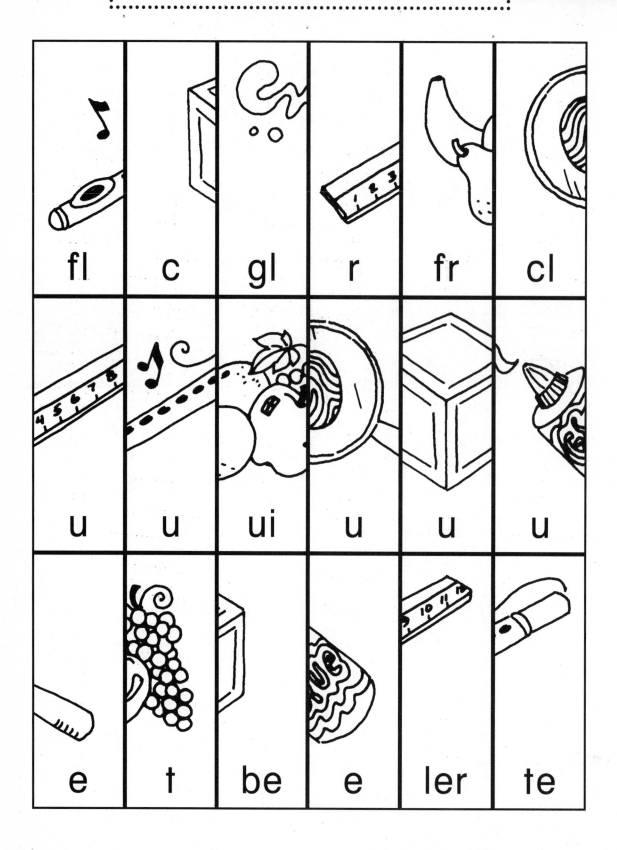

fl	c	gl	r	fr	cl
u	u	ui	u	u	u
e	t	be	e	ler	te

Arrange the pieces to form six words. Glue them in place.

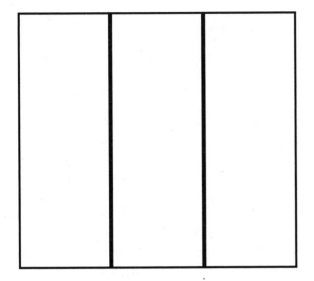

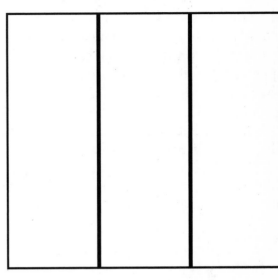

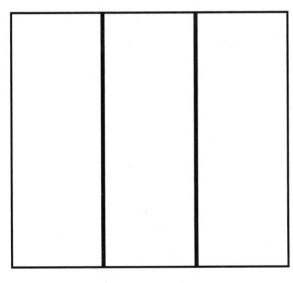

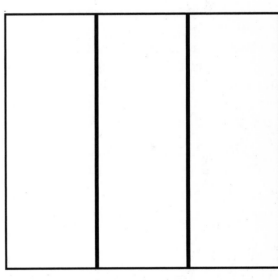

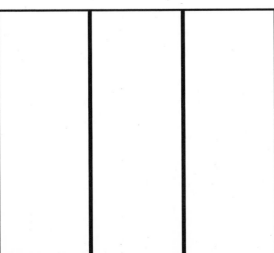

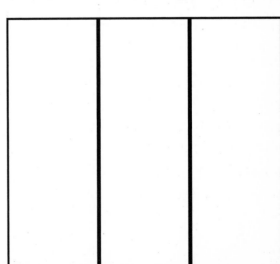

Board Games

Children will enjoy building words and reviewing long and short vowels with the nine reproducible board games on pages 36–45. Additional information about each game appears below. Simply photocopy the game boards and corresponding Word Building Cards (pages 47–58) and laminate them for durability. Introduce one game at a time and review the directions with students. Place the games in a learning center or send them home to give children an opportunity to practice skills with families. These games are designed for two players.

SHORT A:
Hats Off!

Photocopy the game board on page 36 and four sets of short-*a* cards on page 47. Draw an X on the back of the cards with initial consonants. This will help students sort the cards quickly and without looking at them. This game requires small paper squares of different colors. Each player should choose a color.

Variation 1 Make additional cards using the blank card templates (page 58).

Variation 2 Use the short-*a* cubes (page 61) or spinners (page 73) instead of cards.

SHORT E:
Animal Parade

Photocopy the game board on page 37 and four sets of short-*e* cards on page 48. Draw an X on the back of the cards with initial consonants. For playing pieces, you might use beans, chips, paper squares, or buttons.

Variation 1 Make additional cards using the blank card templates (page 58).

Variation 2 Use the short-*e* cubes (page 62) or spinners (page 74) instead of cards.

SHORT I:
It's a Match!

Photocopy game board (page 38) and cut apart the cards. Draw an X on the back of the picture cards.

Variation 1 Pair each word card with its corresponding picture card and place them facedown, side by side. The first player turns over the picture card (the card with an X) and segments the sounds in the word, for example /p/-/i/-/g/. The player then writes the word on a sheet of paper and turns over the word card for verification. If correct, the player keeps the cards and the next player takes a turn. If incorrect, the player places the cards in a discard pile and the next player takes a turn. The player with more cards wins.

Variation 2 Challenge children to arrange the words in alphabetical order and then match the picture cards to the word cards.

SHORT O:
Ollie the Octopus

Photocopy the game board (page 39) and four sets of short-*o* word cards on page 50. For playing pieces, you might use beans, chips, paper squares, or buttons.

Variation 1 Play the game according to the directions on the game board, but add an extra challenge. After a player has formed a word, he or she must name a rhyming word to move to the next wave.

Variation 2 Create additional word cards using the blank card templates (page 58).

SHORT U:
Spinning Fun

Photocopy several copies of the game board (page 40). Do not laminate the boards because players will write on them. Show children how to position a pencil and a small paper clip to use the spinners. Explain that players can spin again if they land on a line. Players can record the same word more than once.

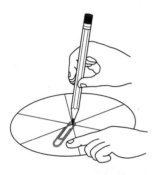

Variation If using the game as an independent activity, explain that children should set a goal of how many words they think they will make all together within a certain amount of time. The player determines in advance how long he or she will play.

LONG A:
Feed Ace the Ape

Photocopy the game board (page 41) and the cards (page 42). Help children assemble their boxes.

Variation 1 To play with two players, each player needs a box and a set of cards. Players shuffle their own cards and stack them facedown. Players take turns drawing ten cards, reading the words aloud, and determining whether the words belong in the box. At the end of ten turns, the player with more cards in his or her box wins.

Variation 2 Challenge children to make additional cards with long- and short-*a* words.

LONG E:
Mystery Picture

Make a copy of the game board (page 43) for each player. This is an independent activity that children can complete in a learning center or at home. To complete this activity, children need scissors, glue, crayons, and a sheet of paper.

Variation 1 Have children guess the picture on the puzzle before assembling it.

Variation 2 Challenge children to list additional words with the long-*e* sound.

LONG I:
Easy as Pie!

Make two copies of the game board (page 44), cut apart the pie pieces, and laminate. Store the pieces in an envelope. Provide students with six-inch paper plates or laminated paper circles.

Variation After players have completed their pies, challenge them to say a rhyming word for each word on their pie.

LONG O AND LONG U:
Word Challenge

Make a copy of the game board (page 45) for each player. Photocopy one set each of long-*o* and long-*u* cards (pages 55–56), cut them apart, and laminate them. This is an individual activity. For a two-player game, see directions below.

Variation 1 Play this game using any combination of Word Building Cards (pages 47–57).

Variation 2 To play Word Challenge, each player will need a game board and a set of long-*o* and long-*u* cards. Each player follows the directions on the game board. The first player to list 8 words wins. Alternatively, the player who forms more words wins.

Hats Off!

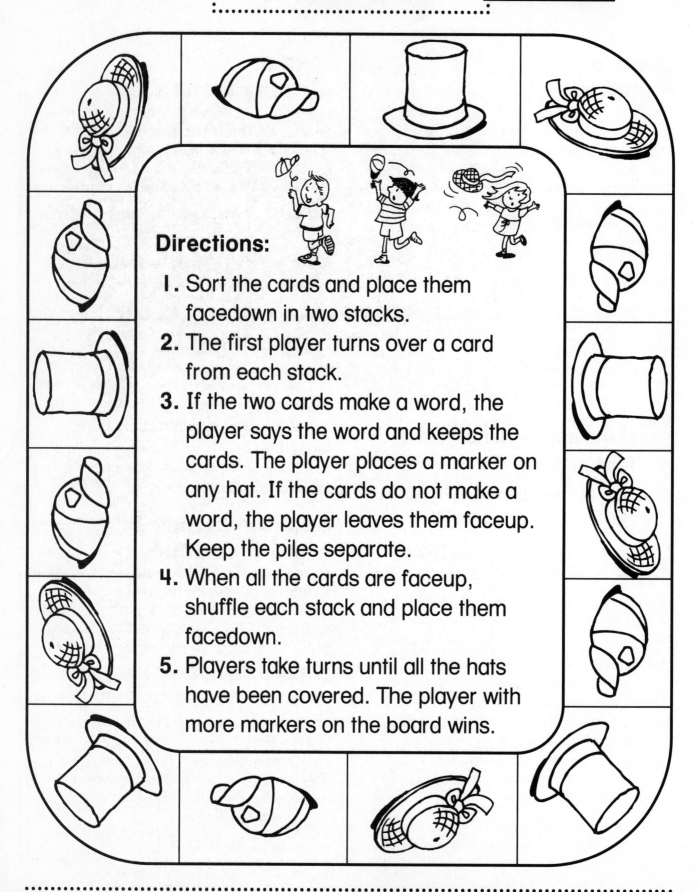

Directions:

1. Sort the cards and place them facedown in two stacks.

2. The first player turns over a card from each stack.

3. If the two cards make a word, the player says the word and keeps the cards. The player places a marker on any hat. If the cards do not make a word, the player leaves them faceup. Keep the piles separate.

4. When all the cards are faceup, shuffle each stack and place them facedown.

5. Players take turns until all the hats have been covered. The player with more markers on the board wins.

Animal Parade SHORT E

Directions:

1. Sort the cards and place them facedown in two stacks.

2. Place the playing pieces on START.

3. The first player turns over two cards.

   If the cards form a word, the player moves ahead one space.

   If the cards do not form a word, the player remains in the same space.

   Place the used cards in two separate stacks.

4. When all cards have been used, shuffle each stack and place them facedown.

5. Players take turns until one player reaches FINISH.

It's a Match!

Directions:

1. Shuffle the cards and spread them out facedown.
2. The first player turns over two cards: one with an X and one without. If the word and the picture match, the player keeps both cards and takes another turn. If they do not match, the player turns over the cards.
3. Players take turns until all cards have been used. The player with more matches wins.

chick	**chin**	**crib**	**dig**	**fish**
milk	**pig**	**ship**	**spill**	**swing**

Ollie the Octopus

Directions:

1. Shuffle the cards and place facedown in a stack. Draw two cards and place them faceup.

2. Player A turns over a card and places it beside the other cards. If the player can create a word with any of these cards, the player keeps those cards and places a marker on Player A's first wave. If the player cannot make a word, the next player draws a card and takes a turn.

3. Players continue to take turns. The first player to reach Ollie the Octopus wins.

Note: If all faceup cards are used, draw two cards and place them faceup.

A　　　**B**

Spinning Fun

Directions:

1. Use a pencil and a small paper clip for each spinner.
2. Each player needs a game board.
3. The first player spins both spinners. If the player can form a word, the player counts the letters in the word and writes it in the correct column. The next player takes a turn.
4. The first player to form 5 words wins.

3-Letter Words	4-Letter Words	5-Letter Words

Fun & Easy Word Building Activities Scholastic Professional Books

Feed Ace the Ape

Directions:

1. Cut along the solid lines.
2. Fold along the dotted lines.
3. Tape together to form a box.
4. Cut out the words on the next page.
5. Read aloud the words.
6. Place the words with a long-*a* sound in the box.

Name

Feed Ace the Ape
Word Cards

✂

		plate
rake	glass	hat
rate	ball	rain
bank	mate	snap
cane	play	mail
made	tan	bat
mad	rat	stray
can	trade	mat
game	band	wait

Mystery Picture

Directions:

1. Cut apart the pieces.
2. Assemble the puzzle by making 6 words with the long-*e* sound.
3. Glue the pieces to a sheet of paper.
4. Color the picture.

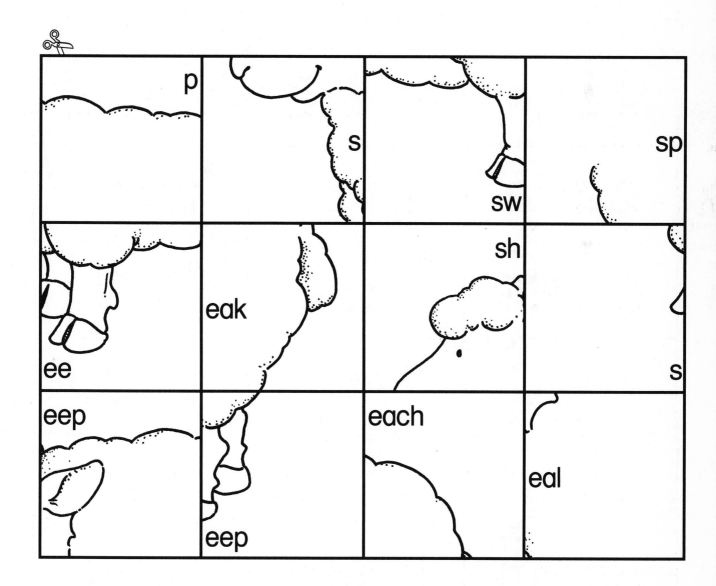

Easy as Pie!

Directions:

1. Cut apart the pie pieces, shuffle, and spread them out facedown.
2. Each player needs a paper plate.
3. The first player turns over a pie piece. The player can keep the piece and place it on the plate, or turn the card back over. The object is to build a complete pie with four pictures.
4. Players take turns until one player has completed a pie.

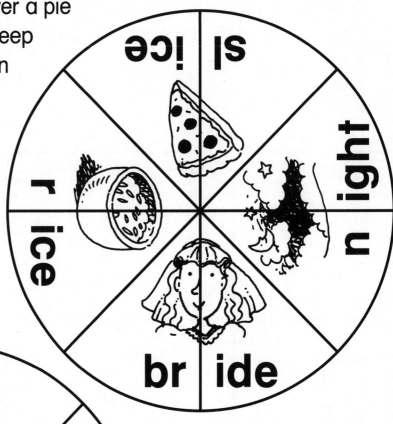

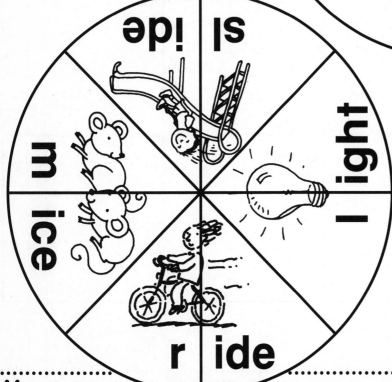

Fun & Easy Word Building Activities **Scholastic Professional Books**

Name _____

Word Challenge

LONG O and LONG U

Directions:

1. Shuffle the cards. Place nine cards faceup on the grid.
   Then place nine cards faceup on top of those cards.
   Place the remaining cards faceup anywhere on the grid.

2. Choose two cards that form a word. Remove the cards
   and write the word on a line. You may move cards to fill
   empty squares.

3. Continue until you have listed 8 words.

1. _____

2. _____

3. _____

4. _____

5. _____

6. _____

7. _____

8. _____

Fun & Easy Word Building Activities   Scholastic Professional Books

Word Building Cards

The Word Building Cards (pages 47–57) are used with many of the board games, but they can also be used independently in a number of ways. The cards are organized by long and short vowels. Simply photocopy them onto paper or oaktag and laminate them for greater durability. Store the cards in an envelope labeled with the long or short vowel. To make additional cards, photocopy and fill in the blank card templates (page 58). Show students the cards and explain how to place them side by side to form a word. Encourage students to use a children's dictionary if they need to check the correct spelling of a word or if they do not know a word's meaning.

Learning Center Practice

Photocopy two sets of cards with the same vowel sound. Store the cards in an envelope labeled with the long or short vowel and leave copies of the Word Recording Sheet (page 95) nearby. Kids can visit the center and form as many words as they can with the cards, then record the words on the recording sheet. Students can use other sets of cards to build more words and add these to their list. As an extension, have students analyze the words on their list and decide how to sort them into the categories on the Word Sort sheet (page 91).

Activities and Games

The games described below are for two players. To make it easy to sort the cards, draw an X on the back of the initial consonant cards.

Pick a Word

Make four sets of cards, either of the same vowel sound or several different vowel sounds. Players sort the cards and place them facedown in two piles. The first player turns over the first two cards. If the player can form a word, he or she records the word on the Word Recording Sheet (page 95) and keeps the cards. If the player cannot form a word, he or she places the cards in a discard pile. Players take turns turning over cards and recording their words. When they run out of cards, players should shuffle and sort the discard pile and use those. When all the cards have been used or no more words can be made, the player with more words listed wins. (Players should not count the same word twice.)

Build a Word

Make four sets of cards, either of the same vowel sound or several different vowel sounds. Players shuffle the cards, stack them facedown, and turn over two cards. The first player turns over one card. If the player cannot make a word, he or she leaves the cards faceup. If the player can make a word, he or she keeps those cards and turns over another card. The player continues taking turns until he or she cannot form a word. The second player turns over a card and tries to make a word using any of the faceup cards. A player can make more than one word in a turn. Play continues until all of the cards have been used or no new words can be made. The player with more cards wins.

Take Six

Make four sets of cards, either of the same vowel sound or different vowel sounds. Players shuffle the cards and stack them facedown. At the same time, each player chooses six cards and places them faceup. Players form as many words as they can, using any combination of the six cards. As they build the words, players record them on the Word Recording Sheet (page 95). Players place the used cards in a discard pile, draw six new cards, and continue in the same way. When they run out of cards, players can shuffle the discard pile and use those. The first player to build 10 words wins. (Players should not count the same word twice.)

s	ack
b	ag
m	an
l	ap
r	ash
c	at

s	ack
b	ag
m	an
l	ap
r	ash
c	at

b ed	s ell	l end	w ent	t est	p et
b	s	l	w	t	p

b ed	s ell	l end	w ent	t est	p et
b	s	l	w	t	p

Word Building Cards

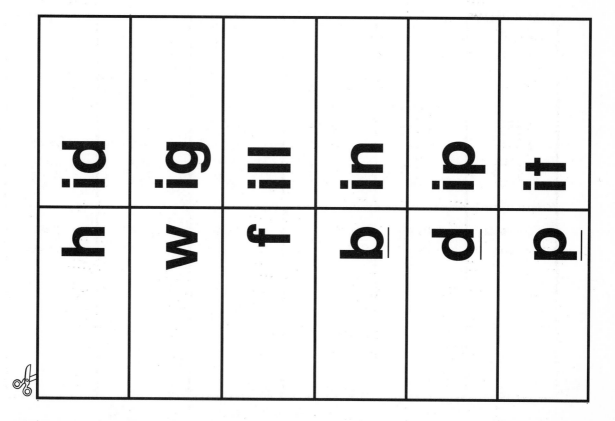

h	id	w	ig	f	ill	b	in	d	ip	p	it

h	id	w	ig	f	ill	b	in	d	ip	p	it

Word Building Cards

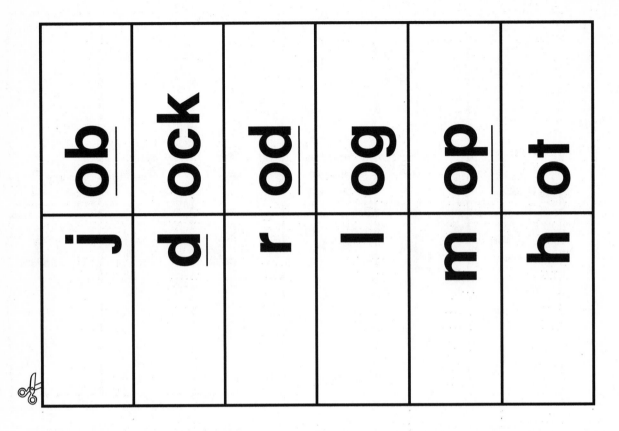

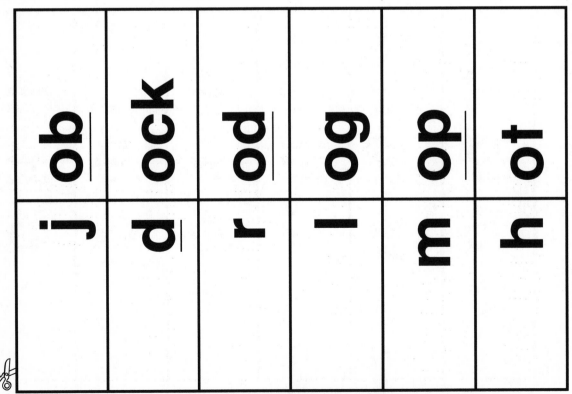

l unch	m ud	j ug	p ump	b un	d unk
l	m	j	p	b	d

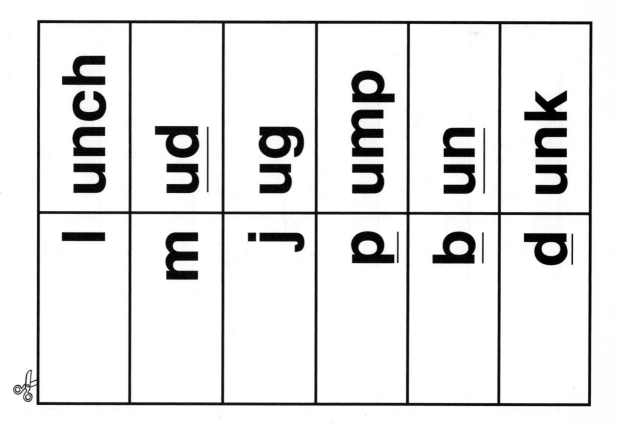

l unch	m ud	j ug	p ump	b un	d unk
l	m	j	p	b	d

Word Building Cards LONG A

t ail	b ake	p ale	m ain	r ate	s ay
t	b	p	m	r	s

t ail	b ake	p ale	m ain	r ate	s ay
t	b	p	m	r	s

Word Building Cards

b each	r eal	t eam	h eat	s eed	d eep
b	r	t	h	s	d

b each	r eal	t eam	h eat	s eed	d eep
b	r	t	h	s	d

ight	ike	ile	ime	ind	ine
r	l	m	t	f	n

ight	ike	ile	ime	ind	ine
r	l	m	t	f	n

oat	oast	old	ole	one	ope
b	t	m	h	c	r

oat	oast	old	ole	one	ope
b	t	m	h	c	r

c	ube
d	ue
r	ule
t	une
s	ure
l	ute

c	ube
d	ue
r	ule
t	une
s	ure
l	ute

Word Building Cards

br	gr	pl	sn	st	tr
bl	cl	fl	sl	sp	sw

br	gr	pl	sn	st	tr
bl	cl	fl	sl	sp	sw

Word Building Cards

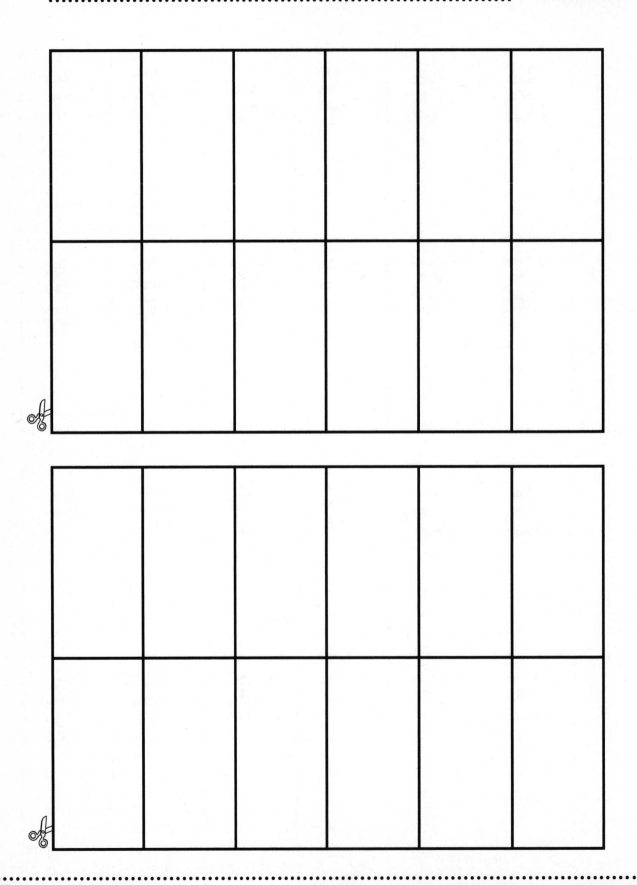

Cubes and Spinners

The reproducible cubes and spinners (pages 61–84) help children review long and short vowels as well as common word families and initial consonants. Children use either two cubes or two spinners at a time—one showing initial consonants and the other showing word families. Children then determine whether they can build a word with the initial consonant and word family shown. Encourage students to use a children's dictionary if they need to check the correct spelling of a word or if they do not know a word's meaning. Children may record words formed on the Word Recording Sheet (page 95) or scrap paper. Using the cubes and spinners gives children a hands-on way to practice reading and blending sounds—strengthening their understanding of the letter-sound relationships, which ultimately improves reading and writing skills.

For an additional challenge, have children use the blends cubes or spinners (pages 71 and 83) instead of the beginning consonant cube or spinner. Create cubes or spinners that show other blends or digraphs using the blank templates (pages 72 and 84).

Assembling the Cubes

To make the cubes, simply photocopy the reproducible page, cut out the cubes, and fold along the dotted lines. Then tape or glue the tabs in place to form a cube. Store them in a small plastic container, basket, or shoe box, labeled with the appropriate long or short vowel. Use the blank cube template (page 72) to create additional cubes.

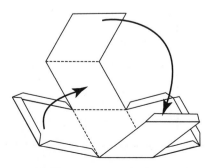

Assembling the Spinners

Photocopy a spinners sheet (pages 73–84) and mount it on oaktag. You might laminate it for greater durability. Photocopy the spinner hands below, mount on oaktag, cut out, and attach with a brass fastener. As an easy alternative, students can use a pencil to hold a paper clip as the spinning hand. Explain to students that they can mark the first space they land on with one paper clip and then use another paper clip for the second spinner. This will make it easier for them to determine if they can form a word with the beginning consonant and word family.

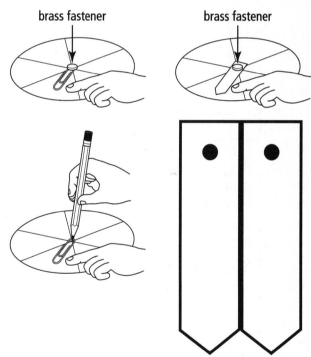

brass fastener   brass fastener

Learning Center Practice

Make one copy of a cubes or spinners page. Assemble the cubes or spinners, label with the appropriate long or short vowel, and place in a learning center. Store copies of the Word Recording Sheet (page 95) nearby. Kids can visit the center and, using a pair of cubes or spinners, form as many words as they can. Have them record the words on the recording sheet. Students can use other sets of cubes or spinners to build more words and add these to their list.

As an extension, have students analyze the words on their list and decide how to sort them into the categories on the Word Sort sheet (page 91).

Activities and Games

The following games are for two players.

Take Ten

The first player tosses the cubes or spins the spinners. If the player can make a word by blending the letters shown, he or she records the word. Players take turns until they have each rolled ten times. The player with more words wins.

Score Four

Make two sets of cubes for different vowel sounds. The first player rolls all four cubes and tries to form as many words as possible. The player then records the words. If the player was able to form four words or more, he or she may roll both cubes again and take another turn. If the player formed fewer than four words, the turn ends and the other player takes a turn. The first player to form 15 words wins. (This game may also be played using two sets of spinners for different vowel sounds.)

Rhyme Time

Make two sets of spinners for different vowel sounds. Each player chooses a set. The first player spins his or her set and tries to form a word. The player records the word. If the player can think of two rhyming words, he or she records them as well. Players continue to take turns. The first player to form 15 words wins. (This game may also be played using two sets of cubes for different vowels.)

Long or Short?

Make one set of long-vowel cubes and one set of short-vowel cubes. To take a turn, a player rolls all four cubes and tries to form words with the letters showing. Before rolling, a player calls out a prediction: long, short, or both. (The player is predicting if he or she will be able to form a word with a long or short vowel or a word with each.) If the player's prediction is accurate, he or she records 1 point. Players take turns until one player has earned 3 points.

Word Spins

Make two sets of spinners (or cubes) for different vowel sounds. Each player chooses a set. At the same time, both players spin their spinners and try to form a word. If only one player is able to form a word, that player earns 2 points. If both players form a word, each player earns 1 point. If neither player forms a word, neither player earns a point. The first player to earn 10 points wins.

Compound Words

To reinforce compound words, write the following words on four blank cubes or spinners (pages 72 and 84). To take a turn, a player rolls all four cubes or spins all four spinners. The player tries to make one or more compound words and records the words. After the player has written the words (or if he or she is unable to form any words), the next player takes a turn. Players take turns. The first player to form 10 compound words wins.

any	dog	place
bath	every	play
bird	fire	room
body	fly	some
butter	fruit	sun
camp	ground	thing
cup	house	under
cake	light	where

Cubes SHORT A

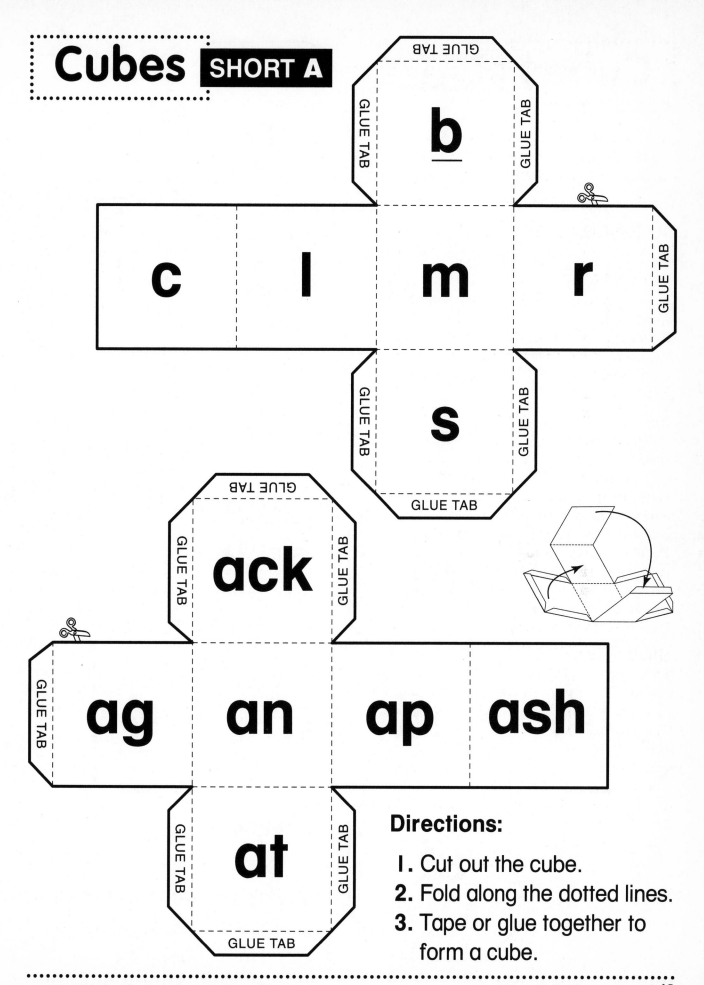

GLUE TAB

b

GLUE TAB   GLUE TAB

c   **l**   **m**   **r**

GLUE TAB

GLUE TAB   GLUE TAB

s

GLUE TAB

GLUE TAB

ack

GLUE TAB   GLUE TAB

GLUE TAB

ag   **an**   **ap**   **ash**

GLUE TAB   GLUE TAB

GLUE TAB

at

GLUE TAB

Directions:

1. Cut out the cube.
2. Fold along the dotted lines.
3. Tape or glue together to form a cube.

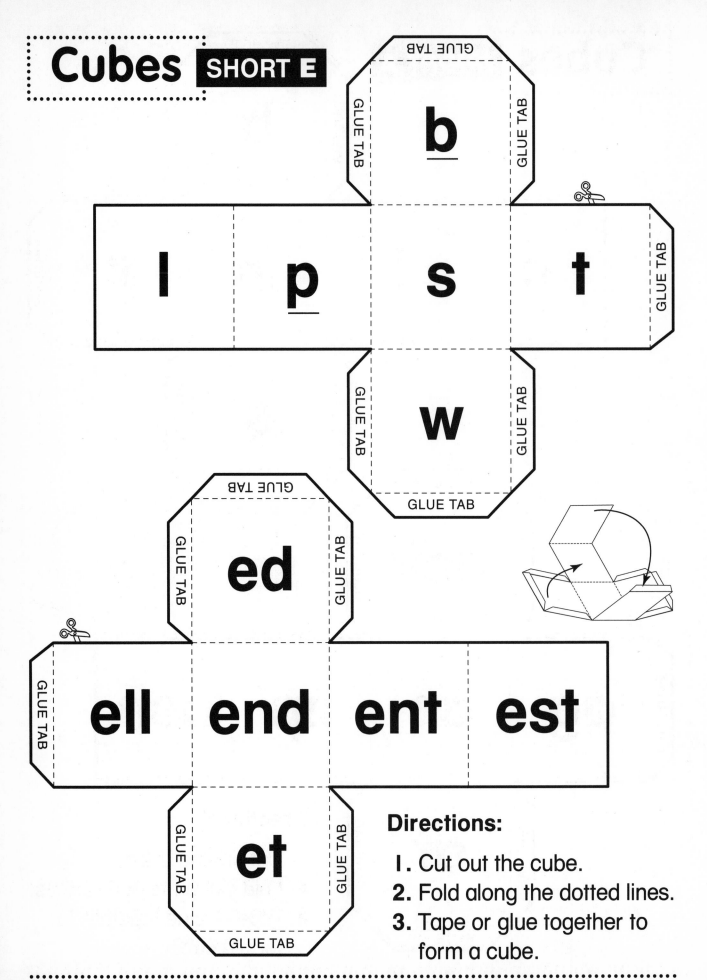

GLUE TAB

GLUE TAB

b

GLUE TAB

l   **p**   **s**   **t**

GLUE TAB

GLUE TAB

GLUE TAB

w

GLUE TAB

GLUE TAB

GLUE TAB

ed

GLUE TAB

GLUE TAB

ell   **end**   **ent**   **est**

GLUE TAB

GLUE TAB

et

GLUE TAB

GLUE TAB

Directions:

1. Cut out the cube.

2. Fold along the dotted lines.

3. Tape or glue together to form a cube.

Cubes SHORT I

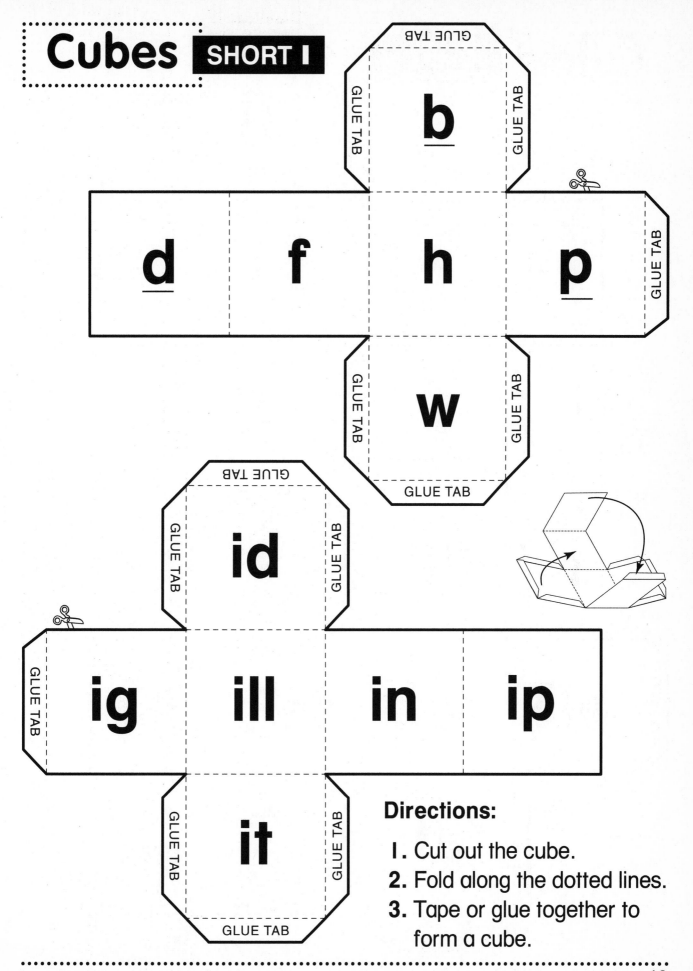

GLUE TAB

GLUE TAB

GLUE TAB

b

d   **f**   **h**   **p**

GLUE TAB

GLUE TAB

GLUE TAB

w

GLUE TAB

GLUE TAB

GLUE TAB

id

GLUE TAB

ig   **ill**   **in**   **ip**

GLUE TAB

GLUE TAB

GLUE TAB

it

GLUE TAB

Directions:

1. Cut out the cube.
2. Fold along the dotted lines.
3. Tape or glue together to form a cube.

Cubes SHORT o

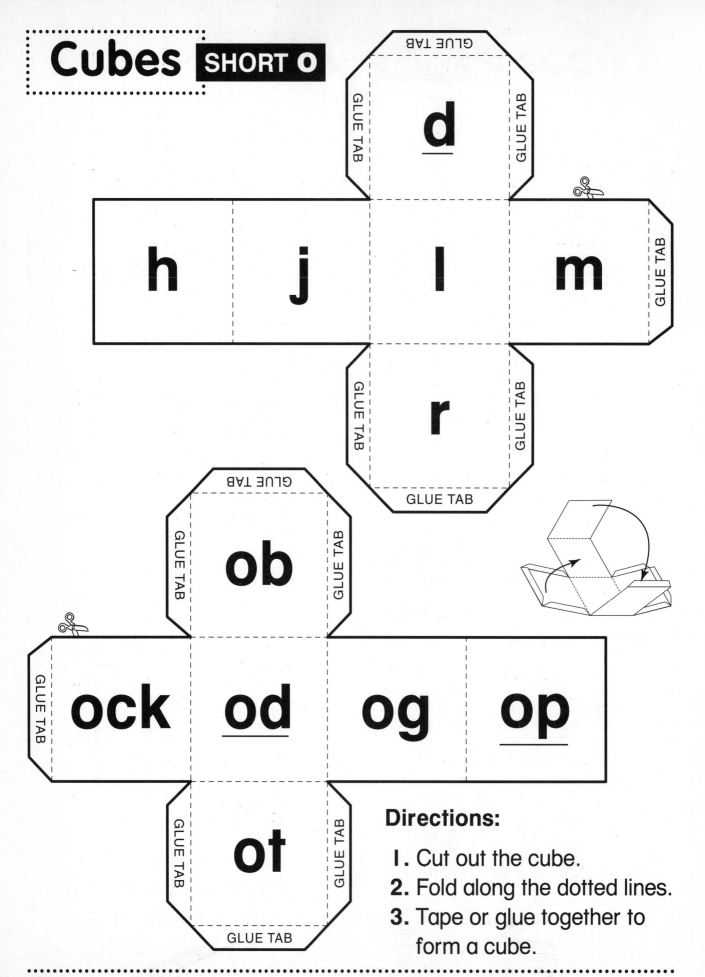

GLUE TAB

GLUE TAB

d

GLUE TAB

h   **j**   **l**   **m**

GLUE TAB

GLUE TAB

GLUE TAB

r

GLUE TAB

GLUE TAB

GLUE TAB

ob

GLUE TAB

GLUE TAB

ock   **od**   **og**   **op**

GLUE TAB

ot

GLUE TAB

GLUE TAB

Directions:

1. Cut out the cube.
2. Fold along the dotted lines.
3. Tape or glue together to form a cube.

Fun & Easy Word Building Activities Scholastic Professional Books

Cubes SHORT U

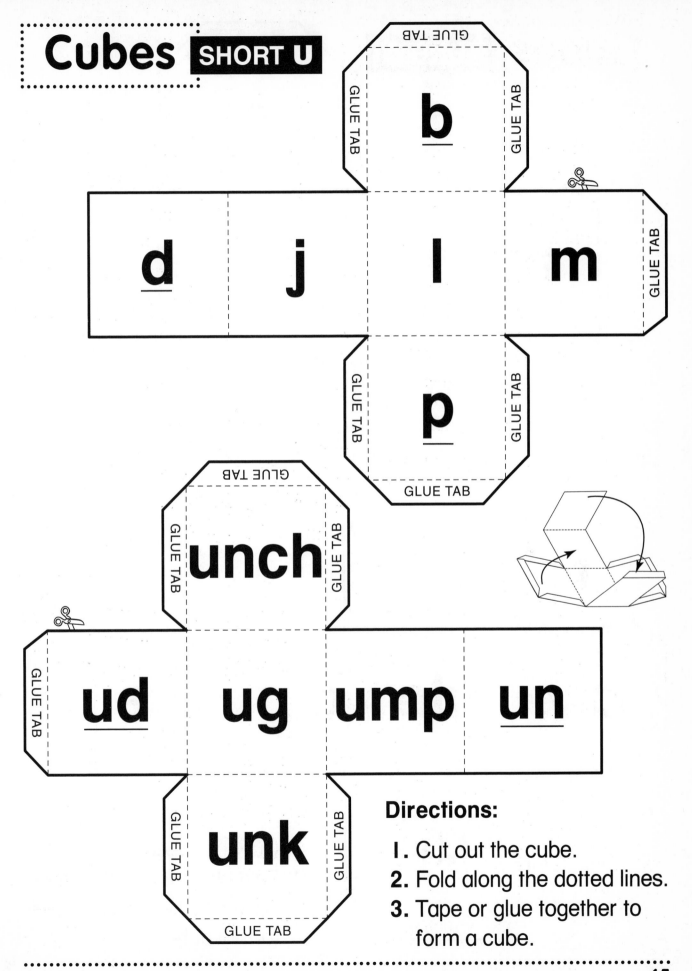

b

GLUE TAB · GLUE TAB · GLUE TAB

d   **j**   **l**   **m**

GLUE TAB

p

GLUE TAB

GLUE TAB · GLUE TAB

unch

GLUE TAB

ud   **ug**   **ump**   **un**

GLUE TAB · GLUE TAB

unk

GLUE TAB

Directions:

1. Cut out the cube.
2. Fold along the dotted lines.
3. Tape or glue together to form a cube.

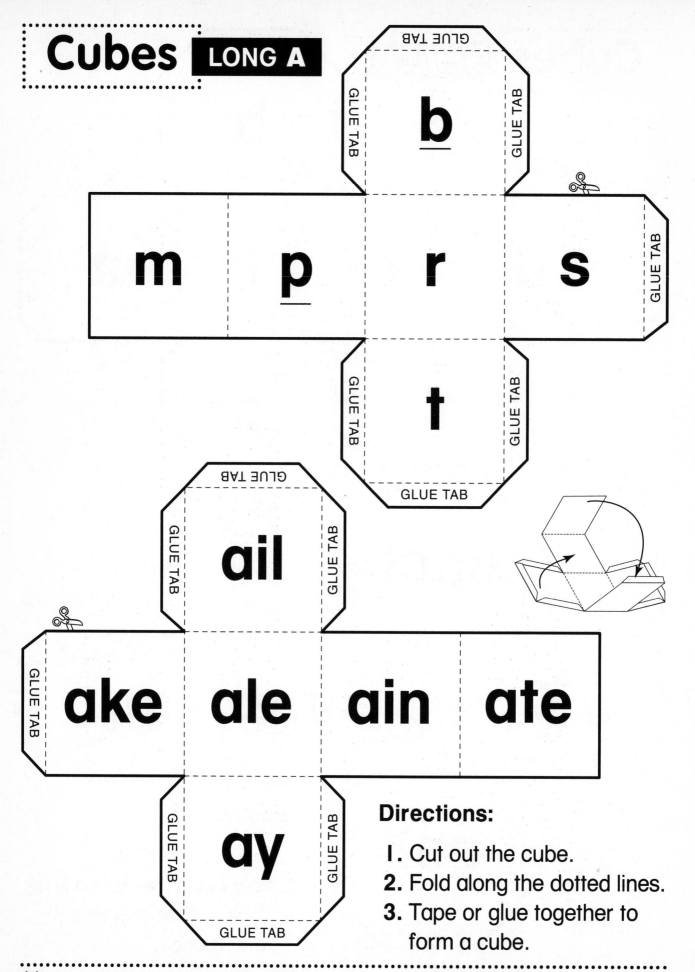

b

m   p   r   s

t

GLUE TAB

ail

ake   ale   ain   ate

ay

GLUE TAB

Directions:

1. Cut out the cube.
2. Fold along the dotted lines.
3. Tape or glue together to form a cube.

Cubes LONG E

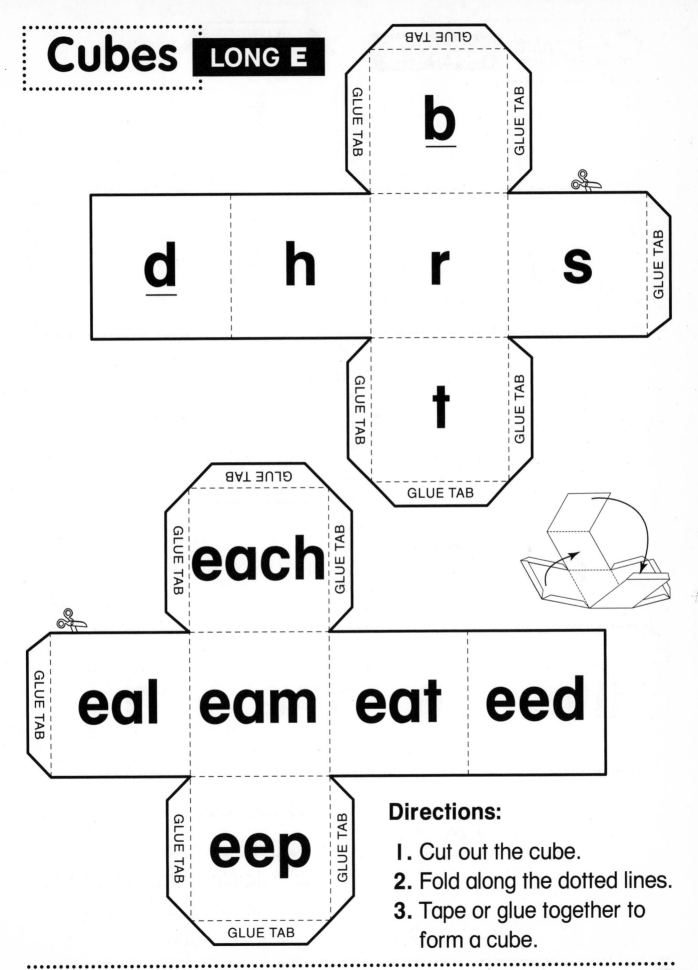

GLUE TAB

GLUE TAB

GLUE TAB

b

GLUE TAB

d **h** **r** **s**

GLUE TAB

GLUE TAB

t

GLUE TAB

GLUE TAB

GLUE TAB

GLUE TAB

each

GLUE TAB

GLUE TAB

eal **eam** **eat** **eed**

GLUE TAB

GLUE TAB

eep

GLUE TAB

GLUE TAB

Directions:

1. Cut out the cube.
2. Fold along the dotted lines.
3. Tape or glue together to form a cube.

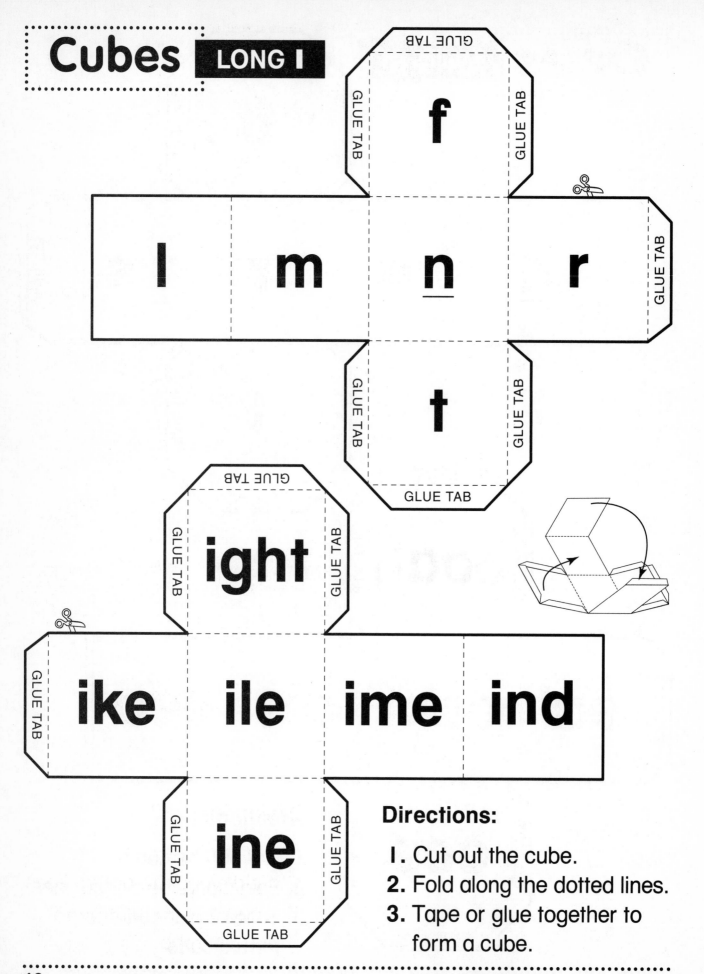

GLUE TAB

GLUE TAB

GLUE TAB

f

l **m** **n** **r**

GLUE TAB

GLUE TAB

GLUE TAB

t

GLUE TAB

GLUE TAB

GLUE TAB

GLUE TAB

ight

GLUE TAB

ike **ile** **ime** **ind**

GLUE TAB

GLUE TAB

ine

GLUE TAB

GLUE TAB

Directions:

1. Cut out the cube.
2. Fold along the dotted lines.
3. Tape or glue together to form a cube.

Cubes LONG o

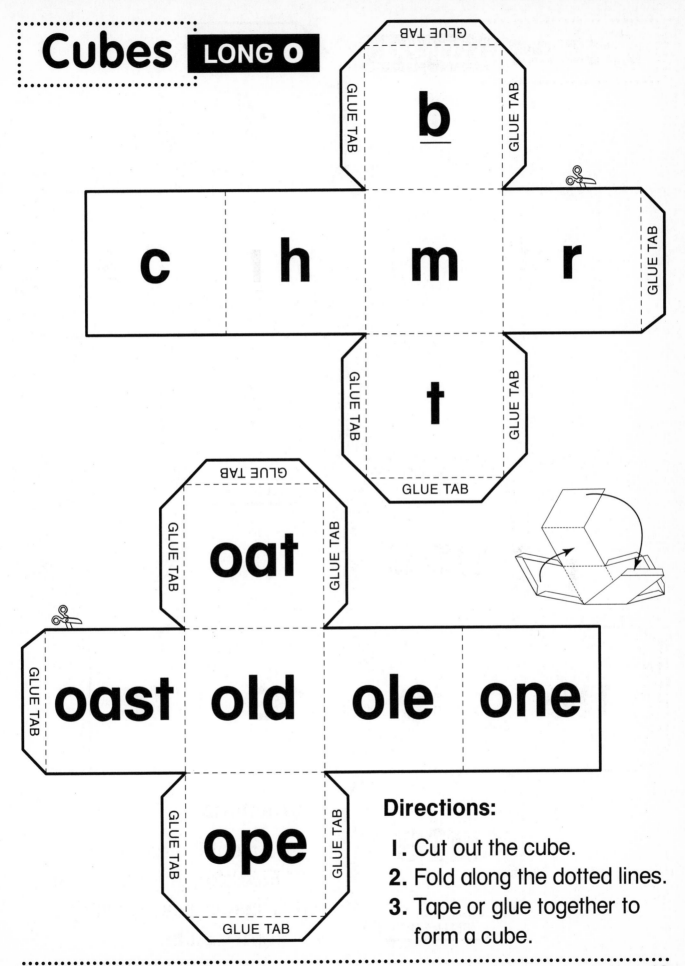

GLUE TAB

b

GLUE TAB   GLUE TAB

c   **h**   **m**   **r**

GLUE TAB

GLUE TAB   **t**   GLUE TAB

GLUE TAB

GLUE TAB

GLUE TAB   **oat**   GLUE TAB

GLUE TAB

oast   **old**   **ole**   **one**

GLUE TAB   GLUE TAB

ope

GLUE TAB

GLUE TAB

Directions:

1. Cut out the cube.
2. Fold along the dotted lines.
3. Tape or glue together to form a cube.

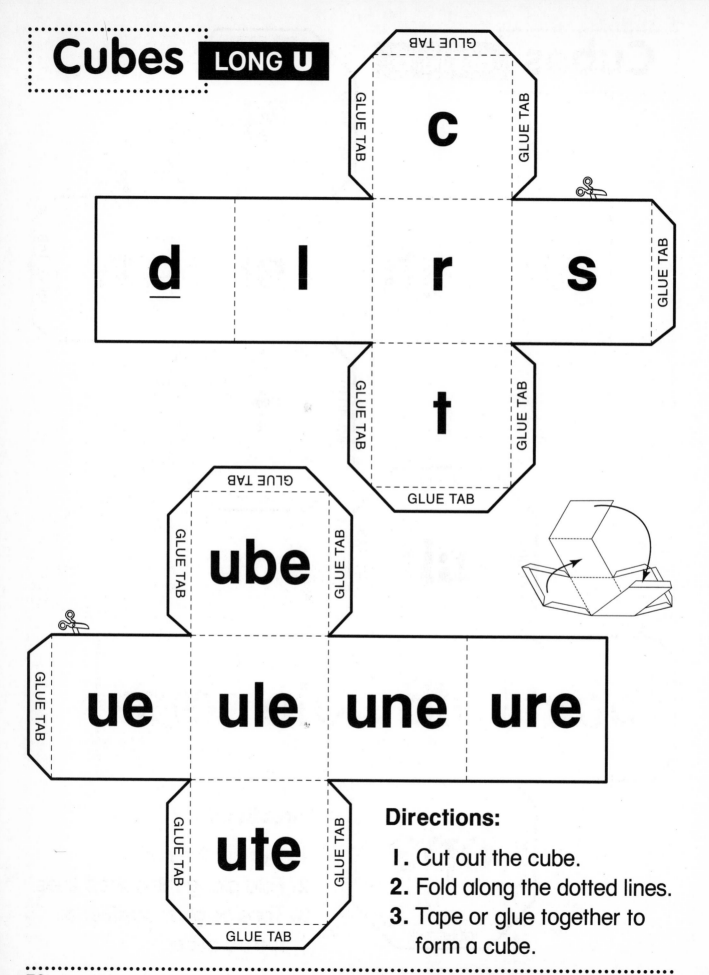

GLUE TAB

GLUE TAB

c

GLUE TAB

GLUE TAB

d l r s

GLUE TAB

GLUE TAB

t

GLUE TAB

GLUE TAB

GLUE TAB

GLUE TAB

ube

GLUE TAB

GLUE TAB

ue ule une ure

GLUE TAB

GLUE TAB

ute

GLUE TAB

Directions:

1. Cut out the cube.
2. Fold along the dotted lines.
3. Tape or glue together to form a cube.

Cubes BLENDS

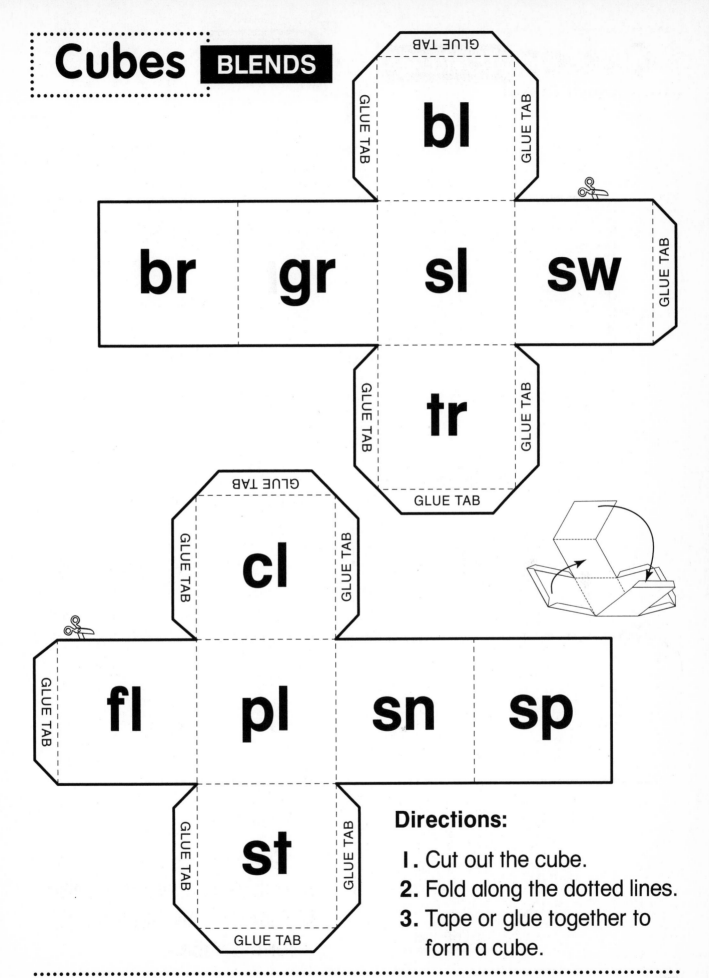

GLUE TAB

GLUE TAB **bl** GLUE TAB

br **gr** **sl** **sw** GLUE TAB

GLUE TAB **tr** GLUE TAB

GLUE TAB

GLUE TAB **cl** GLUE TAB

GLUE TAB **fl** **pl** **sn** **sp**

GLUE TAB **st** GLUE TAB

GLUE TAB

Directions:

1. Cut out the cube.
2. Fold along the dotted lines.
3. Tape or glue together to form a cube.

Cubes TEMPLATE

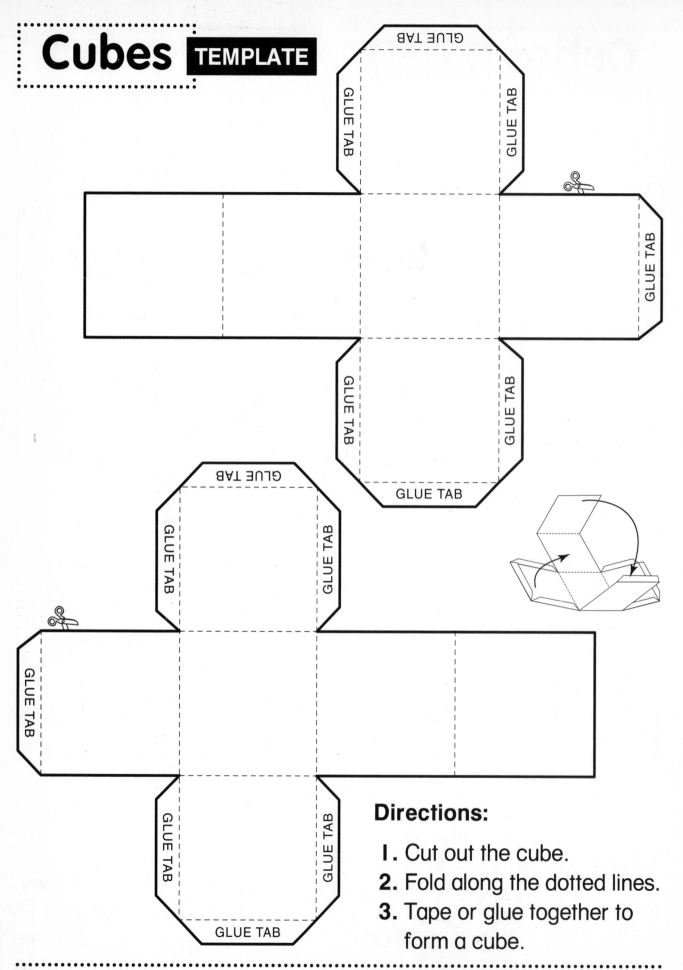

GLUE TAB

GLUE TAB

GLUE TAB

GLUE TAB

GLUE TAB

GLUE TAB

GLUE TAB

GLUE TAB

GLUE TAB

GLUE TAB

GLUE TAB

GLUE TAB

GLUE TAB

GLUE TAB

Directions:

1. Cut out the cube.

2. Fold along the dotted lines.

3. Tape or glue together to form a cube.

Spinners
SHORT A

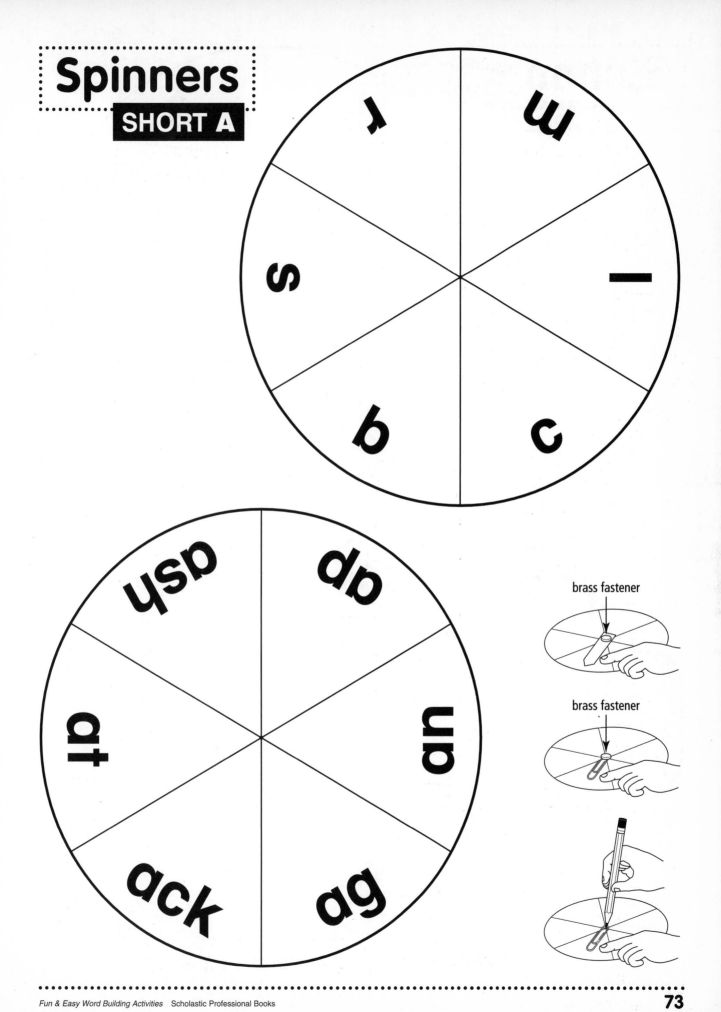

r

m

s

l

b

c

ash

ap

at

an

ack

ag

brass fastener

brass fastener

Spinners

SHORT E

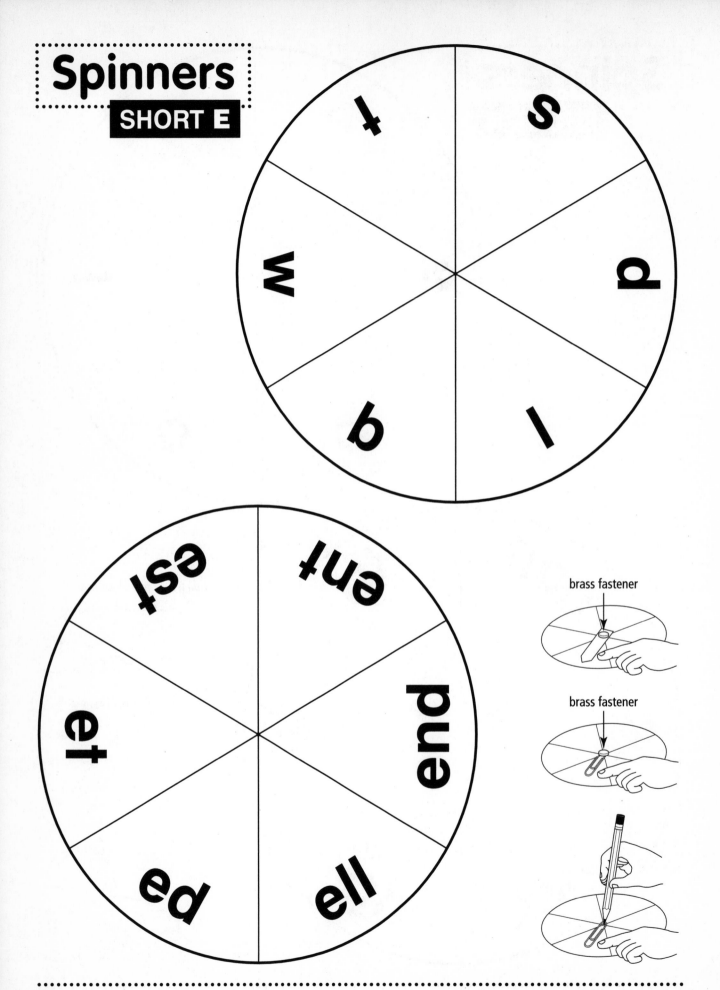

t

s

w

p

b

l

est

ent

et

end

ef

ell

ed

brass fastener

brass fastener

Fun & Easy Word Building Activities   Scholastic Professional Books

Spinners
SHORT I

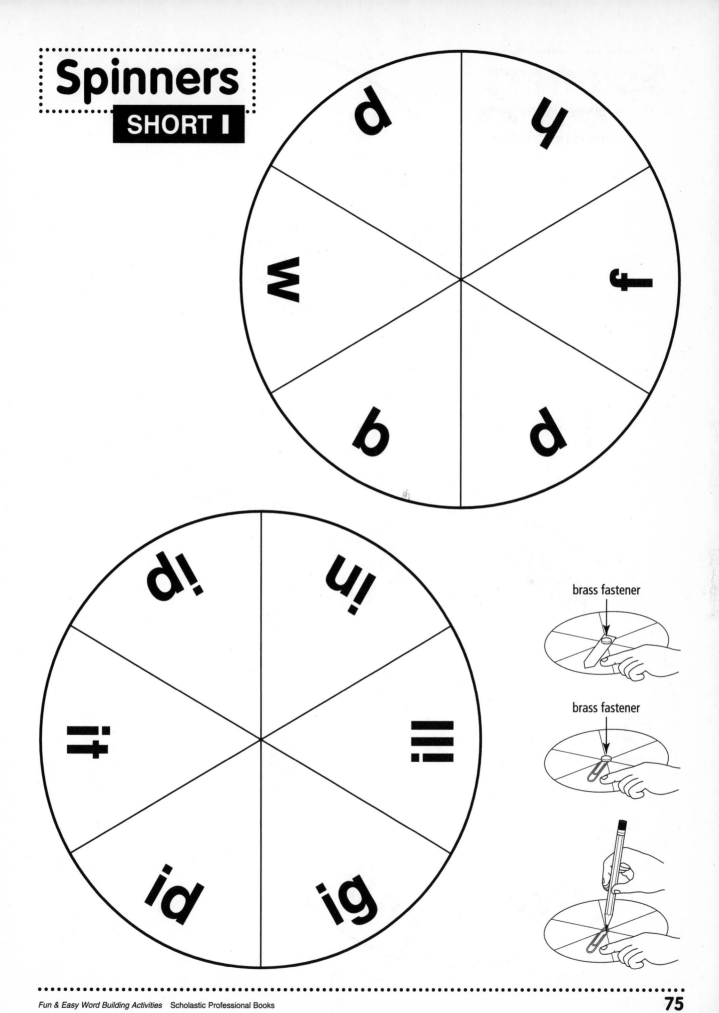

brass fastener

brass fastener

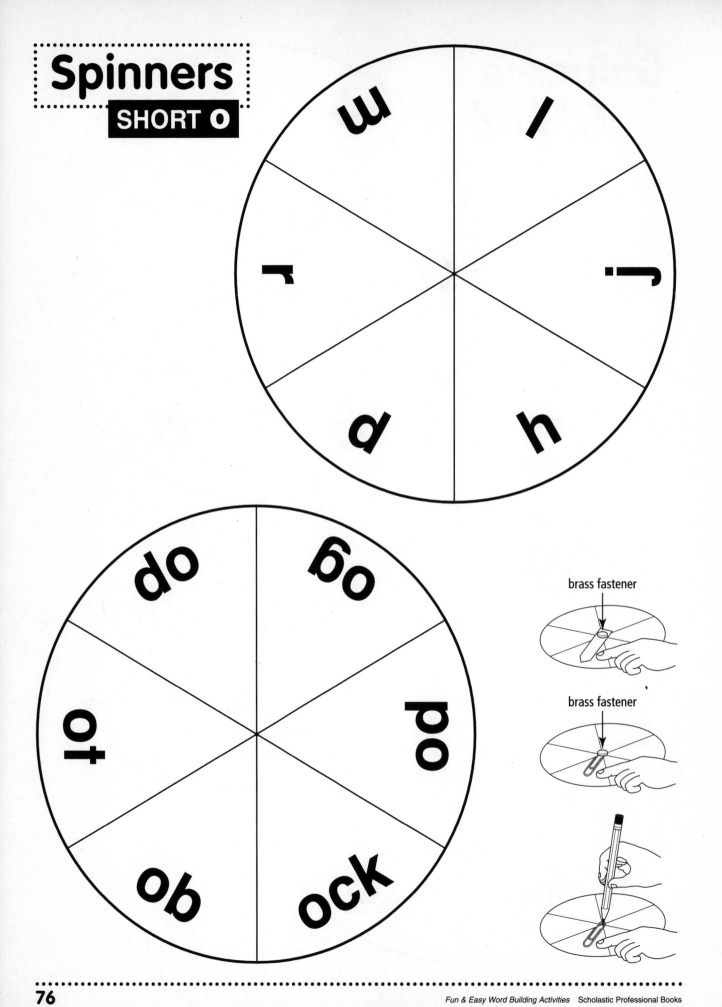

brass fastener

brass fastener

Spinners
SHORT U

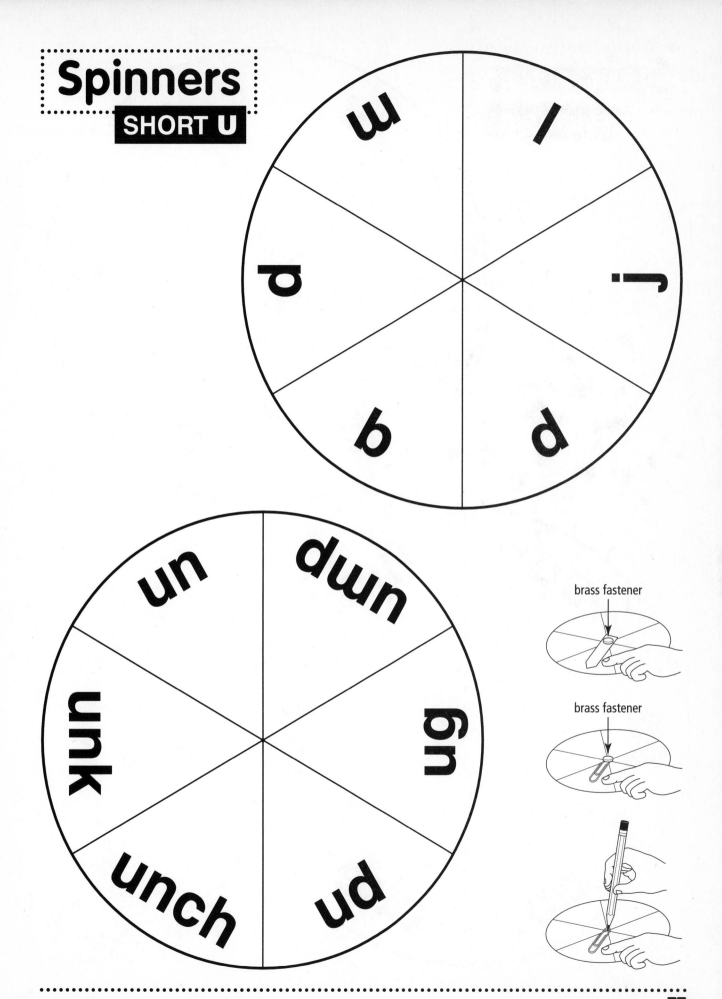

brass fastener

brass fastener

Spinners

LONG A

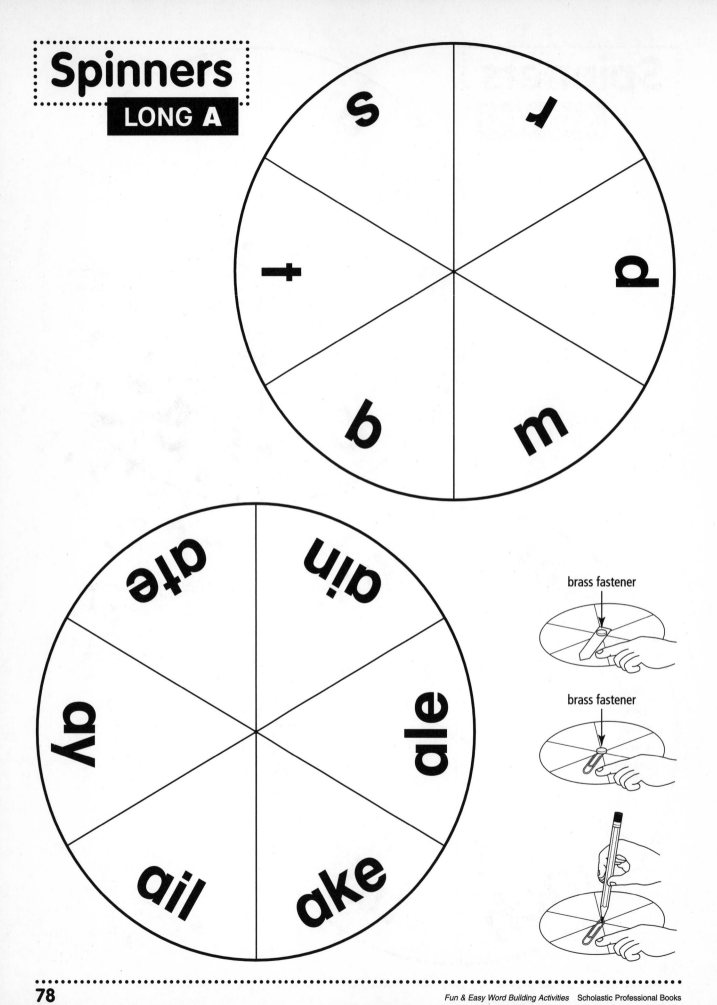

brass fastener

brass fastener

Fun & Easy Word Building Activities   Scholastic Professional Books

Spinners
LONG E

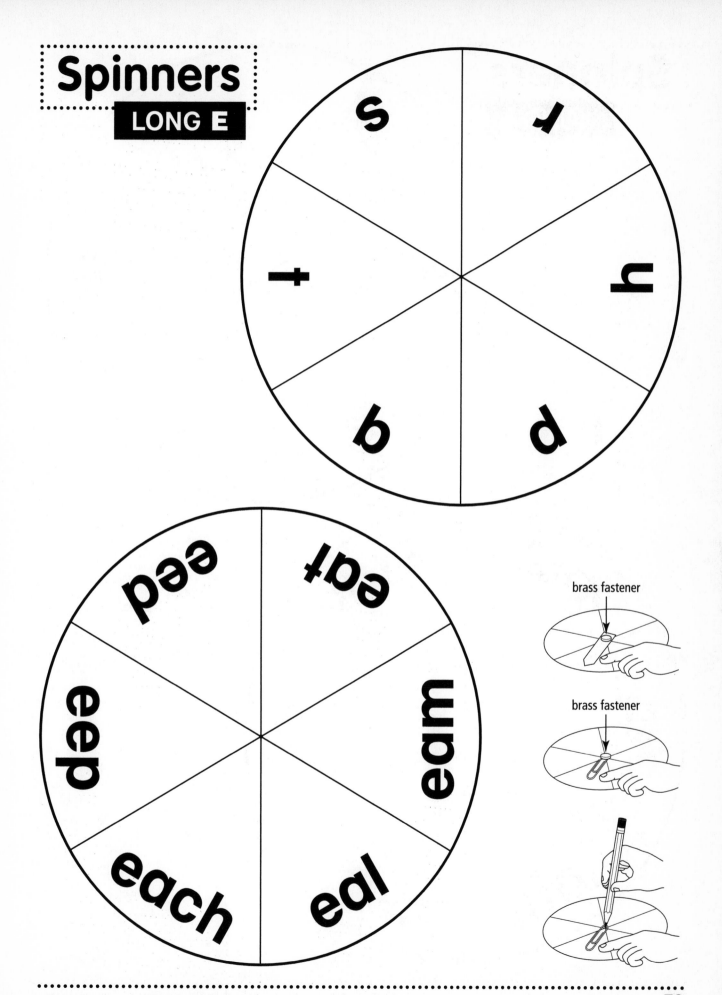

brass fastener

brass fastener

Spinners

LONG I

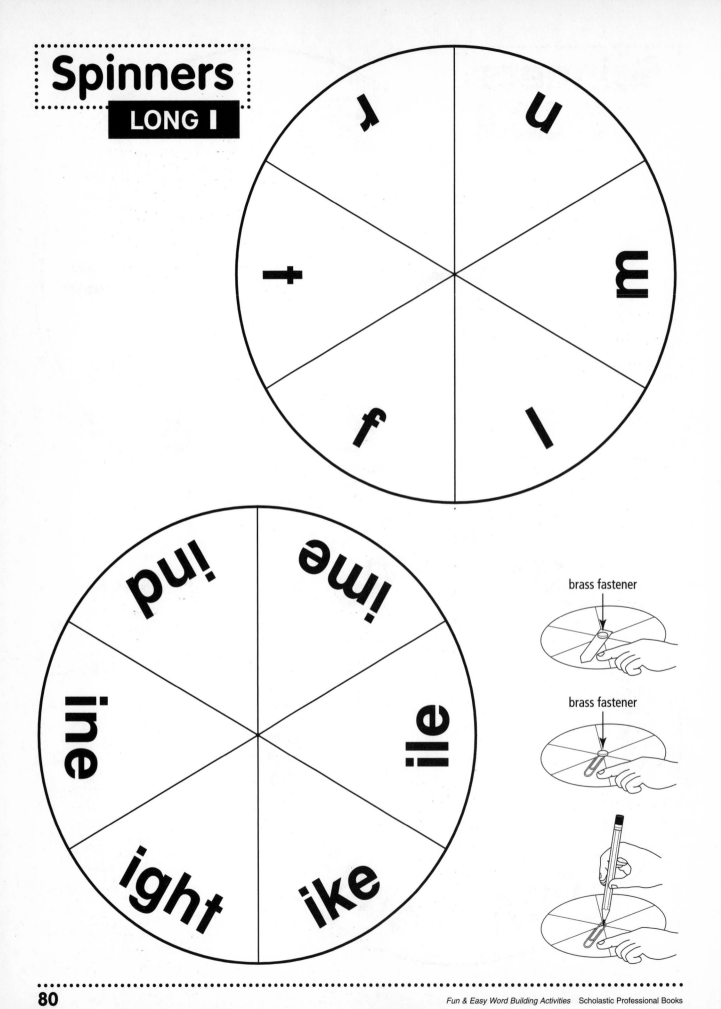

brass fastener

brass fastener

Fun & Easy Word Building Activities Scholastic Professional Books

Spinners
LONG O

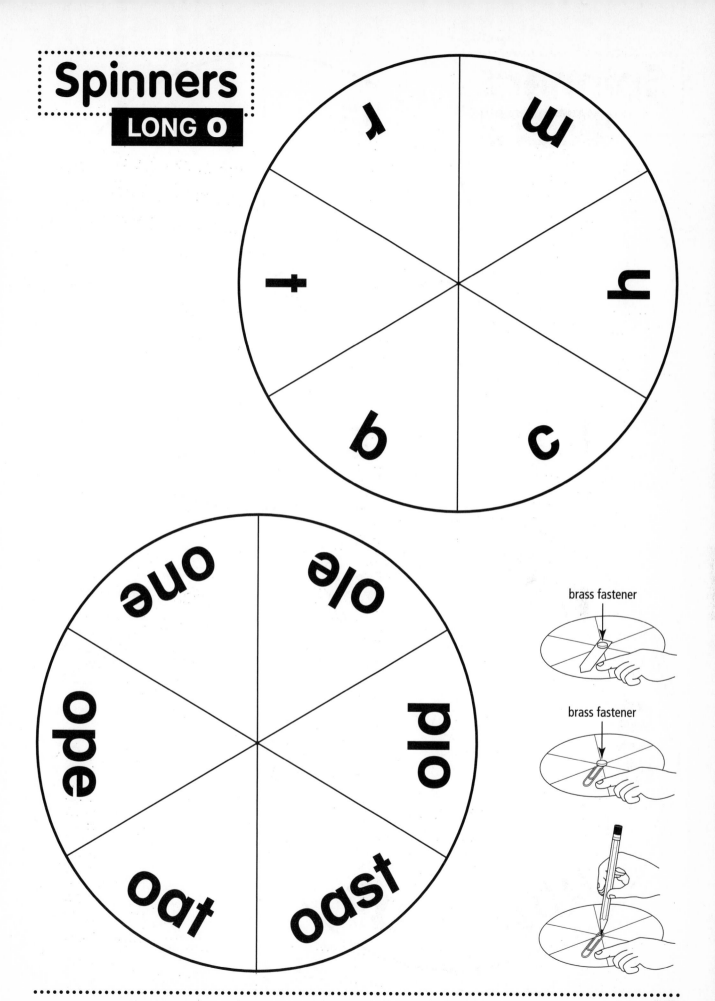

brass fastener

brass fastener

Spinners

LONG U

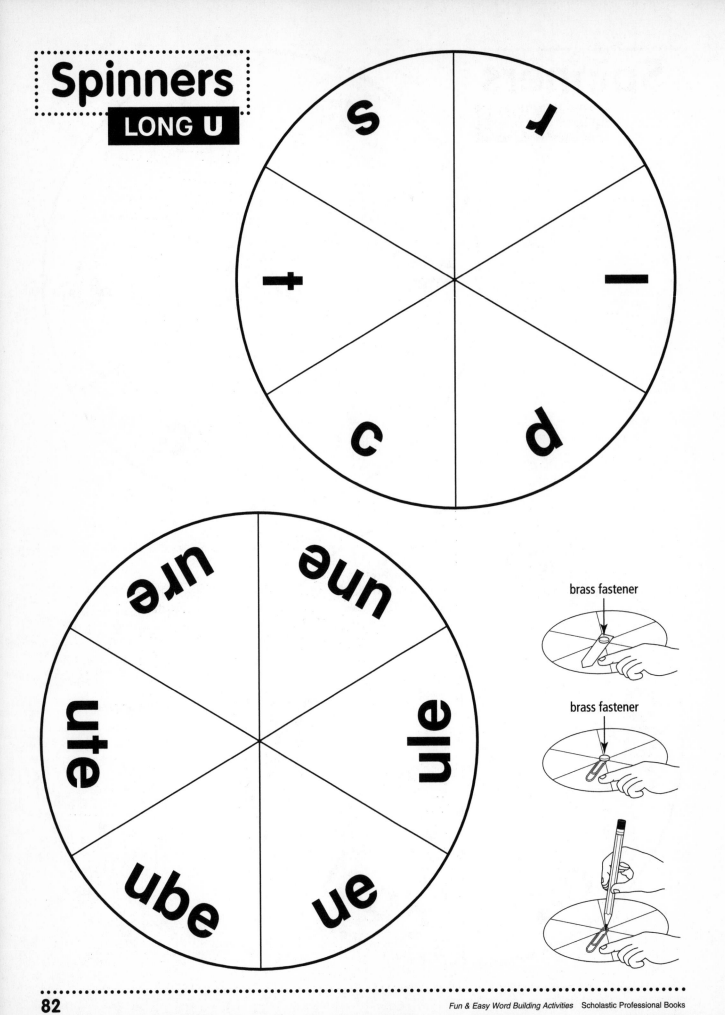

brass fastener

brass fastener

Fun & Easy Word Building Activities   Scholastic Professional Books

Spinners
BLENDS

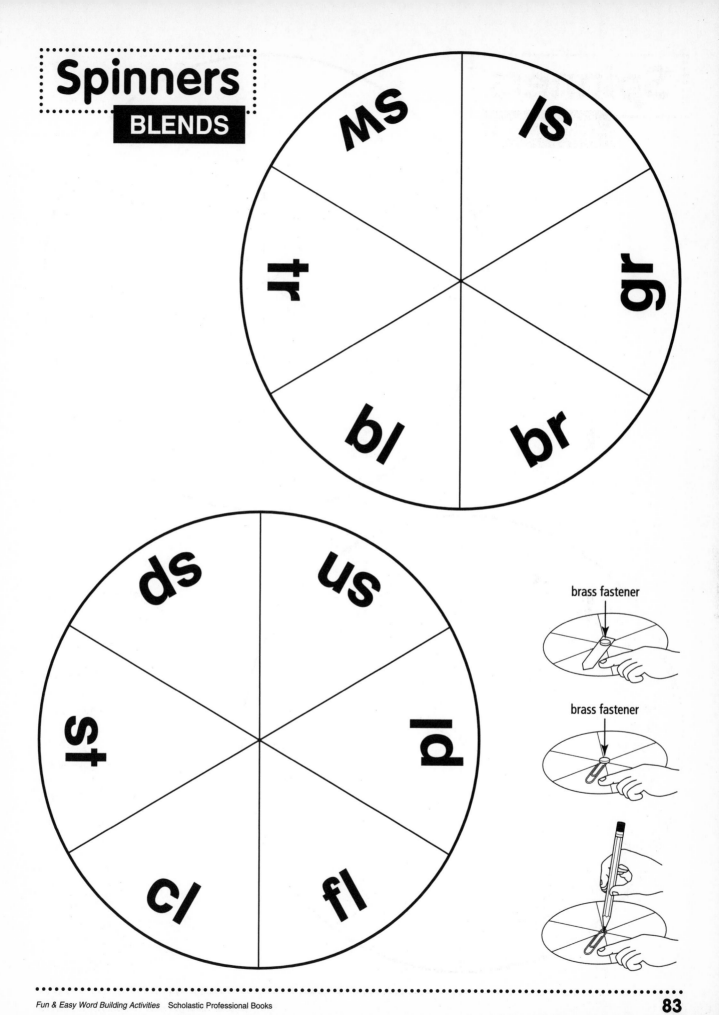

brass fastener

brass fastener

Spinners
TEMPLATE

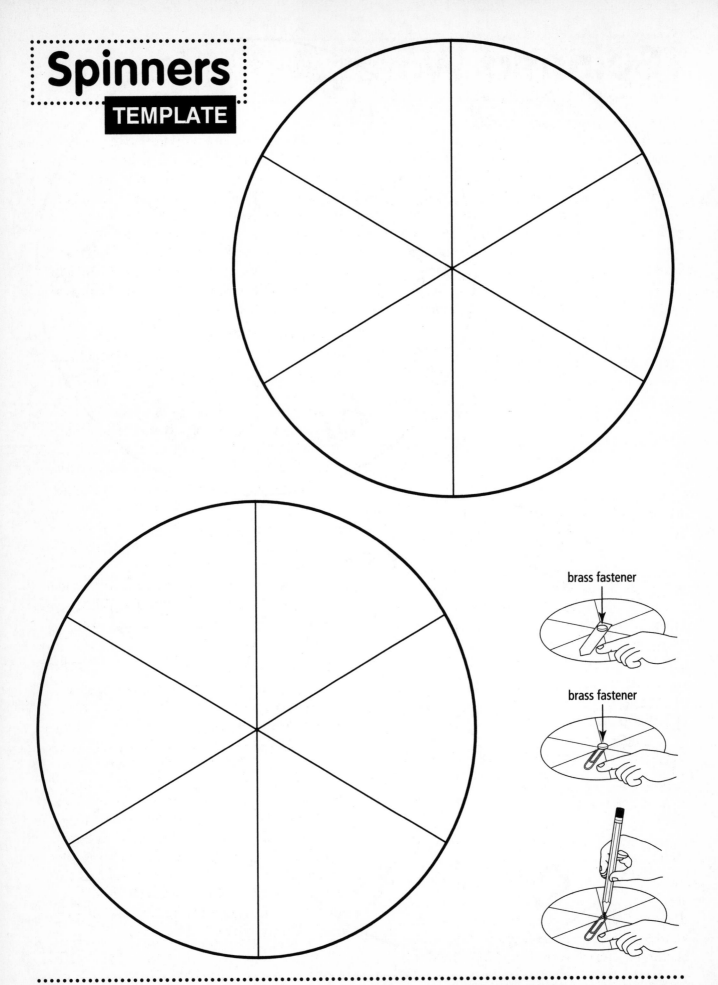

brass fastener

brass fastener

Fun & Easy Word Building Activities   Scholastic Professional Books

Sight Words Activities

Sight words, or high-frequency words, are the words most commonly encountered in any text. Often, these words do not follow regular rules of spelling, so children will not be able to decode them easily—they must simply "know them when they see them." For instance, the word *the* appears about every tenth word in children's books!

There are approximately 600,000 words in the English language, but only 13 of them (*a, and, for, he, is, in, it, of, that, the, to, was, you*) account for more than 25% of the words in print. Children see such words all around them every day. They see them on the walls of their classroom, on signs and advertisements, and on all other types of environmental print. Some children "internalize" these words on their own after repeated exposure, while others need more explicit instruction.

The Dolch Word List

There are several standard lists of high-frequency words, and there is, naturally, much overlap among them. The words in this book are found on the Dolch Word List, a widely recognized list of words that children must learn to recognize on sight. The words on the Dolch List account for more than 50% of the words found in textbooks today. (A second list, Fry's Instant Word List, contains additional words that students need to develop at a high-speed level of recognition.)

Activities and Games

Building Sight Words
For this activity, kids work with groups of sight words that feature common letters. Give each child a photocopy of the letter cards on page 87. Have them cut apart the letters and store them in an envelope. Choose one of the word groups on page 86. Have children remove only the letters that are needed for that group of words. (These letters are listed in bold at the beginning of each word list.) Write the words

on the board and have children manipulate the letters to build the words on the list. After children build a word, have them record it on a list of their own. When they have recorded all of the sight words in that group, challenge them to sort the words by the number of letters, initial consonant, word shape, or other categories. You might have children build additional words using the same group of letters and add these to their list.

Sight Word Bingo
Make a copy of the reproducible Bingo grid on page 88. List 25–30 sight words on the board. Have children write a word from the list in each square. Then call out words one at a time (or ask a volunteer to call out words). Have children place a marker on the square with that word. The first child to mark five words in a row (horizontal, vertical, or diagonal) calls out "Bingo!" For a challenge, speed up the pace.

Word Search
Give each student a copy of the reproducible word search on page 89. Challenge children to find as many words as they can and write them on the lines. You might use graph paper to make additional word searches that feature other sight words.

Silly Sentences
For this activity, you'll need a stack of index cards and markers in different colors. Using a different color for each group, write the following words or phrases on index cards: articles (*a, an, the*), pronouns (*he, she, him, her, you, I, me, they*), adjectives (*big, good, bad*), nouns (*boy, girl, dinosaur, woman*), verbs (*went, goes, is, will*), and prepositional phrases (*to the store, in the house, with his friend*). Using a pocket chart, children manipulate and arrange the cards to form silly sentences. They can create their own cards to add more words to their sentences. Have children work in pairs and read their sentences aloud to each other.

Concentration

Make a set of cards with 20 sight words. On a set of 40 index cards, write each sight word twice (one word per card). Children shuffle the cards and spread them facedown on a flat surface. The first player turns over two cards, trying to make a match. If the cards match, the player keeps them and takes another turn. If the cards do not match, the player turns the cards back over and the next player takes a turn. This game works best with 2–4 players. Make additional sets of cards using other sight words.

Sight Word Groups

a a d l l n w y
a
all
an
and
any
away

a b c e g i k l o o t u y
be
big
black
blue
but
by
like
look

a c d e l m n o u
can
came
come
could

b d n o r w
brown
down

d f i l n n o r u y
find
fly
for
four
funny
you

a e e h l p r v y
every
have
help
here

a e k m s t u y
am
ask
make
me
must
my

e n o r t u w
no
not
now
on
one
our
out

a e e f l p r s t t y
after
play
please
pretty

a d d e i j m n p r u
did
jump
ran
red
ride
run
under
up

a d e e i s w y
as
said
saw
say
see
yes

a e e h i n o o r s t t y
are
at
ate
eat
I
is
she
so
soon
that
the
there
they
this
three

a a d e g i n o o t w
again
get
go
good
in
into
to
too
two

a e e h i o r t w
it
we
what
where
white
who
with

a e i l l n o s t t w y
little
new
want
was
well
went
will
yellow

Letter Cards

a	a	b	c	d	d
e	e	f	g	h	i
j	k	l	l	m	n
n	o	o	p	q	r
s	t	t	u	v	w
w	x	y	z		

Sight Word Bingo

		FREE!		

Fun & Easy Word Building Activities Scholastic Professional Books

Word Search

How many words can you find?
Circle them and write them on the lines.

```
a n b e b i g f o r
n a l o i s v u n m
d p u g g o t n m a
w q e b c n h l k k
e r d c h e r j s e
c f e i i h e i e u
r u n t u p e s e t
d o w n a m a k o n
l w e t t o p m y t
y o u m p l a y a m
```

_____

_____

_____

_____

_____

_____

_____

_____

_____

_____

_____   _____   _____

_____   _____   _____

_____   _____   _____

_____   _____   _____

_____   _____   _____

Review Activities & Reproducible Forms

Word Sort

Word Sort is a follow-up activity that can be used with many of the activities in this book. List the words that were used in the activity or game. Make a photocopy of the reproducible (page 91) for each student. Challenge students to analyze the words and sort them into the different categories: rhyming words, letter switch (words with letters that can be rearranged to make a new word, such as *act* and *cat*), words with short vowels, and words with long vowels. Explain to students what each of the categories means, providing examples.

Variation Give children a similar form with blank columns so that children can come up with their own categories. They might sort words by initial consonant, syllables, number of letters, number of vowels, and so on. Have children work in pairs or small groups and explain their categories to the class.

Word Ladder

In advance, decide which letters you would like children to use in this activity. Make a copy of the reproducible (page 92) for each child. Instruct students to cut out the letter boxes at the bottom of the page. Explain that they should rearrange the order of the letters to try to build different words. They can start at the top of the ladder with a two- or three-letter word and then move down the ladder adding a letter to the word they write in each rung—for example, *it, hit, hits*.

Variation 1 Challenge children to start with a longer word and subtract one letter at a time to make smaller words (*this, his, is*). Or have students rearrange the remaining letters to create each new word (*an, nab, band*).

Variation 2 Have children keep the same number of letters at each rung, but change one letter to form a new word (*bit, bat, mat*).

Spin a Word

Make a copy of the reproducible (page 93) for each student. Each student will need two small paper clips and a pencil to use for the spinners. Write initial consonants, blends, or digraphs on the first spinner and word families on the second spinner. Encourage students to write in pencil so that they can make changes if needed. Explain that students will spin each spinner once. Show them how to position a paper clip and pencil to use the spinner. Students can leave the paper clip in the space they land on and then use another paper clip for the second spinner. If they can form a word, students write the word on the lines.

Review Sheet

Make a copy of the reproducible (page 94) and fill in the boxes at the bottom of the page with letters, blends, and digraphs. Make a copy for each student. Students cut out the boxes, manipulate them to form words, and record the words. Then students follow the directions at the top of the page to circle the longest word, draw a line under the shortest word, and so on.

Variation For a challenge, have children fill in the letter boxes.

Word Recording Sheet

The Word Recording Sheet (page 95) is used with many activities and games. On this reproducible sheet, children list the words that they formed.

Activities Check-Off Sheet

Use this sheet to keep track of the activities each student has completed.

Name _____

Word Sort

Rhyming Words	Letter Switch	Short Vowels	Long Vowels

Name _____

Word Ladder

Directions:

1. Cut out the letter boxes below.
2. Build words up or down:
   Build down—Arrange letters to make a 2-letter word. Write it on the top rung. Then add a letter to make a new word on each rung.
   Build up—Arrange letters to make 5-, 4-, and 3-letter words.

Fun & Easy Word Building Activities Scholastic Professional Books

Name _____

Spin a Word

Directions:

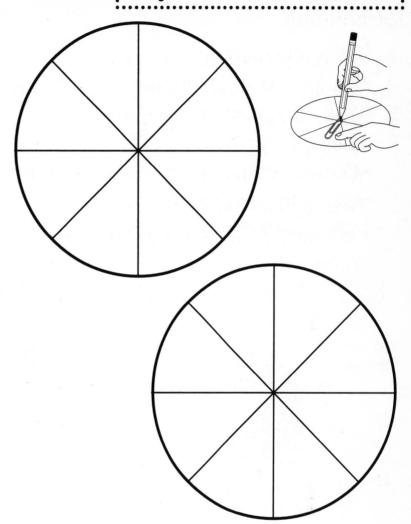

1. Write beginning consonants, digraphs, or blends on the first spinner.
2. On the second spinner, write word families.
3. Spin both spinners.
4. Blend the beginning sound and ending sound together. Do they make a word? If so, write the word on a line. If not, spin again.

1. _____

2. _____

3. _____

4. _____

5. _____

6. _____

7. _____

8. _____

9. _____

10. _____

Name _____

Directions:

1. Cut out the letters.
2. Arrange the letters to make as many words as you can.
3. Write each word on a line below.
4. When you have finished:
   • Draw a line under the longest word.
   • Circle the shortest word.
   • Choose your favorite word. Glue it in the box.

1. _____

2. _____

3. _____

4. _____

5. _____

6. _____

7. _____

8. _____

9. _____

10. _____

11. _____

12. _____

Favorite Word:

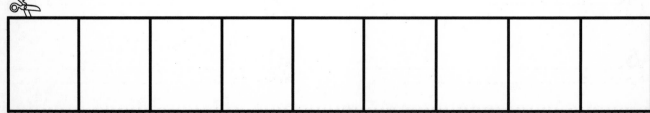

Fun & Easy Word Building Activities Scholastic Professional Books

Word Recording Sheet

1. _____
2. _____
3. _____
4. _____
5. _____
6. _____
7. _____
8. _____
9. _____
10. _____
11. _____
12. _____
13. _____

14. _____
15. _____
16. _____
17. _____
18. _____
19. _____
20. _____
21. _____
22. _____
23. _____
24. _____
25. _____
26. _____

Activities Check-Off Sheet

Write student names and the activity titles on the chart. Check the appropriate box as students complete each activity.

Activity Title

Student's Name

Fun & Easy Word Building Activities Scholastic Professional Books